HOW SOCIAL ENVIRONMENT INFLUENCE BUSINESS STRATEGY

CHANGING BEHAVIOR

JOHN LOK

Copyright © John Lok
All Rights Reserved.

Contents

Preface — vii

Prologue — ix

1. Strategy Function To Organization — 1

2. ● Economic Recession Or Boom How Influences Consumer Behavior — 14

3. Learning Behavioral Economy To Solve Social Challenges — 20

4. Tourism Industry Changing Strategy — 23

5. Airport Service Improvement Strategy — 48

6. Organizational Decision Making Strategy — 52

7. Oil Industry Users Strategy — 57

8. Electronic Vehicle How Influences Future Gas Vehicle Market Changes — 65

9. Why Social Behavior May Influence Organizational Strategy Needs To Be Changed — 71

Preface

Introduction

This book explains why social environment factor may cause any organizations ought need to change themselves organizational strategy in order to avoid consumers number reduces. Why can some businesses experience growth life cycle stage , then going to mature life cycle stage rapidly? Otherwise, some businesses need long time to experience growth and mature life cycle stages. What factors may influence the business may reach growth life cycle stage and mature life cycle stage? Why does some businesses experience decline life cycle stage rapidly ? I shall explain these issues how and why factors may influence any kinds of business develop in their business life cycle stages.

In first chapter, I shall explains why organizations need strategy to be implemented as well as what business model means as well as why business organizations may experience different life cycle stages.

In second chapter,I shall explain that economic recession or boom how influences consumer behavior e.g. the business had been experiencing decline life cycle stage, such as COVID -19 disease occurrence. I shall explain how to apply business development strategy to raise the educational robotic manufacturer sale number.

In third chapter, I shall explain how to learn behavioral economy to solve social challenge as well as why some social challenges may influence customers number .

In fourth chapter, I shall explain what factors influence our tourism industry life cycle stage as well as whether how strateges may influence tourism industry develops.

In fifth chapter, I shall explain why to apply airport service life cycle stage improvement stratey to influence airport service performance.

In sixth chapter, I shall explain what factors may influence managers feel difficult to make decisions in any organizations in general as well as how to help them to avoid the decision making challenges occurrences. I shall indicate how and why computer technological firm merger cooperational strategy may help any technological firms to develop impossible as well as what are the IBM and Apple merger strategic advantages and disadvantages.

In seven chapter, I shall indicate evidences to explain what the factors influence oil industry is experiencing decline life cycle stage.

In eight chapter, I shall explain whether electronic vehicle invention can influence gas vehicle need and how any why it may influence its life cycle stage changes.

In nine chapter, I shall explain what factors may influence public transport service industry reaches life cycle decline stage rapidly.

In ten chapter, I shall explain why and how any management ought spend time to learn organizational life cycle strategies in order to grow up their organizational development more easily when social environment changes.

This book is suitable to any readers have interest to learn how and why what factors may influence any kinds of businesses may experience grow life cycle stage, or mature life cycle stage , even decline life cycle stage from birth life cycle stage in short time or long time.

Prologue

Table of content

Chapter 1 Strategy function to organization

● Explaining what strategy means? p.4-20

● Why does organization need strategist

● Why do SWOT (strengths, weaknesses, opportunitites and threats) analysis can remain a major strategic tool to any organizations?

● What is strategy and strategic management to future managers in organizations?

● What does business development strategy ?

● What is business model?

● What does business climate development strategy ?

● How to implement successful organizational downsizing strategy?

● Business growth strategy

● How whether what obstacles can affect small business growth?

● What can impact on growth strategies on business?

● Why and how can organizational life cycle models influence organizational performance?

● What is the essential elements of life cycle model to assist business development ?

● What can learn from the organizational life cycle theory?

● How to develop organizations in growth stage?

  Chapter 2

● Economic recession or boom how influences consumer behavior

● COVID -19 disease how influence businesses may experience either growing life cycle stage or decline life cycle stage. p.21-31

● How recession influences the role of advertising changes?

Applying business development strategy to raise the educational robotic manufacturer sale number in recession period

● How to develop organizations in growth stage? p.32-45

● How to apply business development strategy to help educational robotic manufacturers to enter traditional education market ?

● Future educational robotic are applied on development teaching maths market

  Chapter 3

Learning behavioral economy to solve social challenges

● Why do some social challenges may influence customers number ? p.46-60

  Chapter 4

Tourism industry changing strategy

● New and old economic theories explain oil is not main factor to influence tourism income

● What are the characteristics of birth life cycle stage to tourism industry ? p.61-95

● What characteristics to space tourism growth stage?

  Chapter 5

Airport service improvement strategy

● How can processes improvement management strategy influence airport service performance? p.96-125

  Chapter 6

Organizational decision making strategy

● Why do managers feel difficult to make decisions? p.126-144

Computer technological firm merger cooperational strategy
● IBM and Apple merger strategic advantages and
disadvantages p.144-160
Chapter 7
Oil industry users strategy
● Reasons cause oil industry experiences
decline life cycle stage p.161-181
● How to raise global gas users need desire ?
Chapter 8
Electronic vehicle how influences future gas vehicle market changes
Factors influence public transport service industry changes p.182-200

Chapter 9
Why social behavior may influence organizational strategy needs to be changed
● Why do organizations need to spend time to learn how may experience different business life cycle stages? p.216-236
● What advantages may bring to the organization if it can attempt to learn how to solve different challenges in different business life cycle stages ?
● What advantages to the organization, if it can know how to experience every business life cycle stage?
● The relationship between learning change management and rapid
reaching mature life cycle
● How to achieve the experience of mature life cycle reaching stage rapidly for product and service ?
Why social behavior may influence organizational strategy needs to be changed

Human Behavioral network job brings social
economic benefits
What does human network job mean
Why human network job behavior may influence economy

Robots take our jobs behavioral and economy influences
Robot job behavior brings economy influences

Intellectual human economic behaviors
What does intellectual human economic behaviors
mean ?
The relationship between social change and human
behavior
How human productive behavior may influence economic development
● New Zealand farmer individual wine productive behavior
● America high technological productive behavior
● China share market investing behavior
Why has any individual country have many people invest share behavior which can influence the country's macro consumption desire?
Can technology influence human shopping behavioral change?
Why and how human behavior may influence the country's economic growth or recession?
Technology how impacts human behavior changing?
How and why employees behaviors may influence economy development?
Robots invention whether they can help organizations to raise efficiencies or inefficiencies?

Why social behavior may influence organizational strategy needs to be changed ? p.201-230

CHAPTER I

Strategy function to organization

● Explaining what strategy means?

What does concept of corporate strategy mean ? Why does organization need corporate strategy ? The reasons may include : reducing cost, making reasonable or the most beneficial decisions or actions, earning above average returns etc. strategy may be a set of key decisions made to meet objectives. A strategy of a business organization is a compenhensive matter plan stating how the organization will achieve its mission and objectives.

A successful strategy may have these four perspectives, a plan, how do I get these; a pattern , in consistent actions over time; a position, it reflect markets, a ploy is a maneuver instead to outwit a competitor, a perspective is a vision, direction, a view of what the company or organization is to become. For minimizes or competitive disadvantage strategy example, company realizes merging with companies advantage . Although, it may not make its market leader , but it may venture into retailing will help it increase profit.

Strategy also may provide a clear understanding of purpose, objectives and standards performance to employees at all level in all functional areas. Usually, every firm competing in an industry as a strategy, because strategy refers how a given objectives will be achieved. For example, computer industry uses a differentation competitive emphasizes innovative product with creative design. For example, coeporate strategy, Coco Cola Inc. has followed the growth strategy by acquition. It has acquired local bottling units to become as the market leader. For function strategy example, pocter and Gamber spends huge amounts on advertising to create customer demand . They aim to maximize resource productivity. It is concerned with developing a distinctive competence to provide the firm with a competitive advantage. Thus, strategy may have different functions. It depends on whether the organization needs what strategy to achieve its objectives or aims.

● Why does organization need strategist

However, any organization needs one or more strategist (s) . strengths are individuals or groups who are primarily involved in the formulation, implementation , and evaluation of strategy. In a limited sense, all managers are strategists. Strategists may include: Consulants, entreprensurs, boards of directors, chief executive officer, senior management, corporate planning staff, strategic business unit level executives, middle level managers, executive assistant titles in any organizations.

Organizations needs outsourced consultants service because many organizations do not have a corporate planning department, owing to small size . Thus, outsource consultancy firm can provide this kind service to them.

Entrepreneurs are promoters who conceive idea of starting a business for getting maximum returns on investment. They are awaiting for an environment change and for an opportunity in the best interest, for example, a biotechnology firm's managing director needs to implement policy formulation in research and development department.

Board of directors are professionals elected may by the shareholders of the company as per rules and regulation of the company act. They are responsible for the general administration of the organization. They are supposed to guide the top management .

CEO is the top man, next to the directors of the board the occupies the most sensitive post, being held responsible for all aspects to strategic management right from formulation to evaluation of strategy.

Senior management from the chief executive to the level of functional or profit centre heads. They are involved in various aspect of strategic management .

Strateic business unit is diivided into different independent units and allowed to form own respective strategies. Middle level managers are operational planners, for departmental plans, as implementers of the decisions as well as executive assistant is a person who assists the chief executive in the performance of his duties in various ways, e.g. data collection and analysis, suggesting alternative, where decisions are required. preparing briefs of various proposals, projects and reports, helping in public relation. All of above positons may be any organizations' role in strategic plan.

● Why do SWOT (strengths, weaknesses, opportunitites and threats) analysis can remain a major strategic tool to any organizations?

It is one straight formed methodology for making a structured analysis of strengths and weaknesses into core competences and core problems by using the core-competence tree and the current reality true. The core competences and core problems are then linked into a plan of action aimed at preserving the organization's core competence. It supposes that any organizations ought have internal strengths and weaknesses both. So, if the organization has strengths , it also ought have weaknesses. Any organization, itself ought have ability to control or avoid or threaten its any weaknesses cause as well as finds any method to arise strengths to bring itself competitive ability. Otherwise, due to external environment factor, it can not control. So, it supposes any organization can not control any opportunities ot threats when they will occur or encounter to influence weaknesses, eliminate all weaknesses that do not satisfy the following criteria.

The weaknesses that do not satisfy the following criteria: The weaknesses must exist over a period of time can not be a one-time phenomenon, the weakness must be expressed in undesirable terms, the weakness must be under the firm's control or influence . So, any firm hopes to eliminate weakness, it depends on how it causes significant damage to the company. For example, when one firm discovers that the project ought may be finished within five months. But, after four months, it discovered that this project can not be finished, if it hopes staffs can cooperate to finish this project before five months, it needs to find whether what its main weaknesses are influenced this project will delay, e.g. lack of innovation, lack of growth, insufficient attractive profits to excite staffs to work. Hence , SWOT is a strategic management tool, it consists of the analysis, decisions and actions, an organization undertakes in order to create competitive advantages. However, the next phases of the strategic management process is external and internal organization's strengths and weaknesses analysis, by conducting an external analysis , an organization also needs to identify the critical threats and opportunities in its competitive environment. It also needs to examine who external competitive environment influences its business develops in long term.

In fact, any organizations need to make the most reasonable strategic choice with vision, mission, objectives and the external and internal analysis of its external environment influence. Hence, the strategic management process may include this steps:

From vision to mission to objectives to (SWOT analysis, external analysis and internal analysis both) to strategic choice (the most reasonable choice) to strategy implementation to achive competitive advantage . So, any organizations must need to spend long time to gather data to analysis whether which it has actual internal strengths and weaknesses as well as what the present external envioronment brings opportunities and threats to influence its business development, if it hopes to implement effective strategic plan. So, it seems that SWOT ought be one step to any organization's strategic plan management process. Thus, managers have responsibilities to help their organizations to try to " fit" the analysis of externalities and internalities, to balance the organization's strengths and weaknesses as well as environmental opportunities and threats . For one car sale manager hopes to find methods to solve its car low sale problem. In the SWOT analysis, it may have these questions: Why does the performance of the car firms in the same motoe sale service industry, operating under the same competitive environment? Which tangible resources of the high performance motor sale service firm provide sources of competitive advantage and subsequent superior motor sale service firm performance? How do the identical tangible resources actually create value for a motor sale service firm in the motore service industry and provide the motor sale service firm with source of sustainable competitive advantage?

Thus, assumption of questions are needed in order to help organizations to attempt to seek the main factors influence their short or long objectives can not achieve in the SWOT analysis process. Then, they can evaluate the different factors to make the reasonable analysis to decide whether which is the main factor to influence their objectives can not achieve satisfactory . Then, they can revise their errors as well as find the most reasonable or the most right solutions methods to achieve their objectives more successfully. Because some factors influence the business actions its objectives sucussfully. They may include: poor organizational behavior, e.g. worse staff performance, working attitude, lazy , they do not enjoy or feel bore to so their work, they feel salaries are not reasonable; poor strategy, e.g. the business ought not expand more branches at this moment rapidly, the business ought chose partnership , it is more suitable to compare sole trader formation, the organization ought advertise to raise its brand awareness to let public to acknowledge etc. wrong strategy implementation. So, SWOT stragegy role may also help any organizatons to revise whether they have errors in order to find the most reasonable factor to cause their poor performance or low profit etc. effects.

● What is strategy and strategic management to future managers in organizations?

Are they understood and recognized? However, I believe that the development of organizational strategy depends on understanding the perceptions of their managers on what strategy and strategic management actually is. The identifications of perceptions of future maangers will need have some insights , opinions and knowledge on the organization's this matter reflect the efficiency and effectiveness of the strategy related learning proces in themsleves organizations. So, I believe that, the manager needs have enough knowledge about how to manage the kind of business if he/she hopes to become the organization's proficient leader, for example, one supermarket business CEO ought own part supermarket operation experience, when he/she has practised supermarket operation experience to know how to manager teams cooperation efficiently, e.g. cashiers, food promoters, food warehouse delivers, grocery shelf putters, fresh fish and fruit pick up keepers, family daily e.g. tooth paste, bath daily products, washing cloth products shelf putters staffs. Then, the supermarket store manager ought have excellent managing ability to manage the supermarket different sale teams to cooperate efficiently. So, owing the kind business managing experience to the manager will be one main factor to influence the business to grow or expand more successfully. Thus, how management develops strategies to guide how an organization conducts its business and how it will achieve its target objectives . The manager himself/herself managing ability and the organization's target objectives can be achieved, they will have close relationship . It is management's responsibility to adjust negative conditions by undertaking strategies defense and managerial approaches that can overcome adversity. However, the essence of the good strategy-making is to build a positive strong and flexible enough to provide successful performance despite unforeseeable and unexpected external factors.

Thus, the five tasks of strategic management may include as below: First step, developing a vision and a mission. It means that any firm ask is " What is our business and what will it be ? What is our business and what will it be ? " Managers need to develop the next five to ten years a clear mission to his organization needs to achieve. A clear mission can establish the organization's future effects and outlines " Who we are, What we need to do and where we are going ? "

Next step. setting objectives, or mission statements can achieve performance targets more easily . Objectives serve as for tracking an organization's performance and progress . A desired performance can pushes an organization to be more incentive, how to improve its financial performance, and its business position. Objectives may have short, middle and long time. Objectives may have two kinds. One is financial objectives, e.g. measures as earning's growth, return on investment and cash flow. The another is strategic objectives, it provides consistent direction in strengthening a company's overall business positon. They relate more directly to a company's overall competitive situation, such as growing faster than the industry's average and making gains in market share.

Then, crafting a strategy step, it is a SWOT analysis to find how to achieve organizational mission. Thus, strategy will be the most important part in order to let the organization to achieve its short, middle and long objectives more easily. For motor industry example, global competitor is competitive environment to motor manufacture industry, if the motor firm can not innovate its any kinds of motors, then it can not attract car buyers to choose its cars to drive. So, in vehicle manufacturing strategy aspect, if the vehicle firm hopes to raise its any kinds of car sale number. How to innovate to manufacturer " new design cars" which may be one important factor to influence any one motor firm sale growth in success. Then, car industry strategy ought concentrate on how to improve the car design to be more attractive. It is " the growth of motor design techniques concep strategy to any nowadays car manufacturers ". It seems that is SWOT analysis to car industry internal strengths and weaknesses analysis have more influential to compare external environment opportunities and threats to any one car manufacturer seller ought not only consider how to train car salespeople sale skill. They ought consider how to provide the useful opinions from car customers' design feeling to car manufacturers, in order to assist them to attempt to design any the most attractive car design to satisfy car buyers' needs in this global car competitive market. So, car design will be one important factor to influence car sale growth. Strategy ought focus on " how to innovate car design" to satisfy car buyers' car design pursue.

On conclusion, any kinds of businesses must have themselves characteristics or features. So , management ought need to consider how themselves business features or characteristics to decide the most reasonable ot the most right strategy implementation in order to achieve their objectives or missions more easily. So, lacking any strategic organizations ought be difficulty to achieve their missions or objectives to compare owning any strategic organizations in nowadays business environment.

● What does business development strategy ?

An effecting business development strategy ought have these five steps: The first step is market analysis. Who are your clients , knowledge of your market? Second step is how to adopt for each penetration, your business needs to learn how to adopt for each group of clients, your first need to review your own capacbility. It is important that you are realistic and honest with yourselves over where clients truly sit, learn how to classify your clients into similar groups relative is the scale of the opportunity. Third step learns how to review your performance , market matrix to plot your results to help you determine your market penerstion. In addition, it will help you then discuss and consider various strategies for growth. By potting your clients you will get a sense of where your strengths and weaknesses are against the opportunity that total market offer.Fourth step learns how to consider alternative growth strategies on the market matrix. The final step , you need to consider these questions in order to decide whic is the most effective strategy for your business. For example, which model is the most (least effective? Why? which model work best for line managers, HR are finance, why? How might we most effectively progress from one model to the most reasonable questions?) Then, you will need to decide how to launch new services, new products, opening new markets, how accessing new geographic territories.

● What is business model?

It is logic and provides date and other service evidences that demonstrates how a business creates and delivers values to customer. It also help how to predict revenues, costs, and profit with the business enterprise delivering that value. How does on build a competitive advantages and a super normal profit ? How the enterprise creates and delivers value to customer, and receive payments to profit easily .

In essence, a business model is a conceptual, rather than financial model of a business. An effective business model may help you to decide how to create value for customers, receive payment to profit more easily. For example, driving factors include knowledge economy, the growth of the internet and ecommerce, the outsourcing and offshoring of many busness activities, and restructuring of the financial services industry, i.e. the enterprise simply need to learn packed its technology and intellectural property into a product which it sold, either as a discrect item or as a bundled package.

The existence of electronic computers that allow low cost financial statement modeling has facilitates of assumptions about future revenues and costs. Also, the concept of a business model has no established theoetical in economics or in business studies. Economic theory assumes that trades take place around tangible products : intangibles are the best. For example, inventions are often assumed to create value naturalty and enjoying protection of patients, firms can capture value by selling patients to market, i.e. the publisher sells the another's books, the books can help it to earn high level of royalty income. In economic theory explains the publishers can create intengible value, e.g. royalty as well as tangible value, e.g. selling books.

However, business mides are necessary features of market economies, it is consumer choice, transaction cost, amongst consumers and producers and competition. It meets invention and consumer wants of new product value need and the opportunity to satisfy their needs. So, good designs are likely to be highly siutational, and the design process is likely to involve processes. New business models can both faciliate and represent innovation. For example, in te sport apparel business, sponsorship is a key component of today's business models, Nike, Reebook, Adidas and other sponsor football and rugby clubs and teams as well as royalties from sale sport related products, e.g. sport shoe, spot cloth. Moreover, business models must be over times as changing markets , technologies and legal structures to adopt the kind of business market change.

A business model achieve the logic the useful and reasonable data and evidence thst support a value decision for the customer. In practice, successful business models very often become to some degree, "shared" by multiple competitors in possible . Strategy analysis is this an essential step in designing a competitive business model, i.e. low cost strategy for newspaper advertising (including classifieds) helps cost of generative content is easy to replicate and of many different geographically separate newspaper market in the world. So, when a country's newspaper publisher may have a differentiated and hard to initate low cost advertising strategy, but it can achieve the same time effective and efficient. Its business model will be successful in newspaper publishing industry. Hence, it seems that business model will be any businesses' essential part in their growth strategies. If the business has none a successful business model, it will not have successful growth strategy consequently.

Growth strategy is different to business development strategy, why ? Growth strategy will mark afresh start, by having all economic actors in the private sector activity and dynamically undertake efforts to promote growth with a determination to take on challenges, when the business feels that it is the right time to grow its business. Otherwise, business development strategy is not the businessmen's feeling whether it is the right time to develop its business . It is essential part to any business expects to start.

● What does business climate development strategy ?

What are the different between business growth and business development and business climate development strategy ? In fact, business growth strategy refers any businesses start up in beginning from earlier stage to nature stage of life cycle. Otherwise , business development strategy must not start up from beginning. It is common on the middle stage, the business hopes to develop its market share or new market to be more. So, it needs to find whether what its SWOT in order to develop its new niche market more successfully.

Hence, it brings this question? Business climate development strategy is on the beginning or middle or mature stage in life cycle? I shall explain as below:

A business climate development strategy means that it is one targeted policy tools appear to favour medium-sized , well established industrial enterprises over younger, small enterprises with high-growth potential operating in the services. Hence, any governments may attempt to follow the business environment to implement any methods to help small size businesses to grow up easily in the beginning stage. In general, implement to business elimate development strategy challenges may include: Lacking of coordination means that there is a disconnect between business and innovation support policies on one hand of investment localization on the other. However, to solve this challenge, governments may encourage these organizations to participate , such as technical centres, laboratories and training facilities can act as catalysts for industry, sector aggregation and support the establishment and specialized investment zones. Hence, the difference between business climate development strategy and the other both strategies. Business climate development strategy is any countries' governments attempt to follow the business environment at the moment to find the most effective methods to help any small size businesses to grow up more easily in the beginning stage.

How to implement business climate development strategy more successful? The key recommendations may include: To emergy from the workshop was further strengthened in an effort to close the policy gap and create synergies between programmes. Building on the experience of regional investment centres, the context points would identify an small middle size's (SMS) organization, and help enterpreneurs to establish a network of SMS bisiness centres across the country. So, they could not as single -window contact points, storing and channelling information abour all the government's SMS business programmes. However, a successful business climate development strategy should build on the analyzed risks and rewards of informal business operations and aim at modifying the behavior of economic agents (enterprises, employees and customers) through a combination of incentives and penalties.

Any governments may attempt to develop a number of measures to promote and suport innovation and upgrade technology in the private enterprise sector. In order to enhance business climate development strategy to implement in success. They may include: establish a system of communication and cooperation between the institutions and private sector organizations operating in the area of technological upgrading, innovation, financial, technical standards, public education and training . It would be useful to conduct an evaluation of the enterprise Europe network's impact in order to learn from the lessons of the country's more successful sector-specific centres. It is the national strategy for innovation, technology upgrading and investment encouragement. Finally, a critical element in an effective innovation strategy is the establishment of links between support services and programmes and access to funding to support any business founder hopes to develop himself business in success in order to adopt business environment climate change more easily.

However, in general, small or medium size business will encounter these challenges when they hope to adopt the business environment climate change to grow their businesses more easily. Their challenges may include: The lack of economies of scale, which limits their ability to invest in fixed capital and technological development, proportionally higher costs,, which increases the impact of the legislative and regulatory framework, information lacking which limit access to external financing, limited resources for internal training and human capital developments. In general, any governments need to help the new business to solve these challenges in order to develop business climate development strategy more easily. They may include: innovation technology centres and networks as well as financial support for innovative SMES. Hence, business climate connection with larger foreign enterprises through active government support, the policy objective is to enhance SME access to international markets, skills development, finance and technology to any businesses' beginning stage in order they can grow up their businesses to nature stage in their business life cycle successfully.

Hence, whether which firms hace real need to get government's business climate development strategy assistance. I believe that the government needs to assume the firm has these challenges in order to ensure that the firm can achieve the requirement to get this business climate development strategy assistance. They are needed to assume on basic these factors: A company must grow and pass through all stages of development or die in attempt, second the models fail to capture the important early stages in a company's origin and growth. Third, instead of annual sales , although some mention number of employees whether it is more or less factor, government can not ignore other factors to decide whether the firm can be accepted to implement climate business development strategy assistance, such as value added, number of locations, complexity of product line and ratio of change in products or production technology etc. factors to decide whether the firm is suitable to be accepted to get business climate development strategy assistance from the government in order to avoid waste time and resource and money to desing any kind of business climate development strategy to assist the firm to develop in the beginning.

● How to implement successful organizational downsizing strategy?

What are the effects of downsizing on organizational performance? What is the most right time to downsizing to the organization ? When one organization has grown to the bigger size , e.g. more revenues, this year than last, a larger workforce, greatest market share, downsizing strategy ? If an organization did not grow, it was viewed as stagnating and upproductive in the non-growth life cycles stage, it implements downsizing strategy to influence its performance to be worse.

Organizational downsizing strategy is one part of the management of an organization and designed to improve organizational efficiency, productivity and/or competitiveness. Downsizing means to reduce organizational size, e.g. staffs number reduces expenditure reduces, cost reduces . Downsizing is an intentional set of activities, it differentiates from loss of market share, loss of revenues or unwritting loss of human resources organizational decline. Also, downsizing usually reductions in personel, such as transfers outplacement, retirement incentives reduction, byout packages, layoffers. This reductions in personnel may occur in one part of an organization, but not in other parts, e.g. in the production function, or not in the engineering function. Finally, downsizing may effect work processes, e.g. fewer employees are left to do the same amount of work, and this has an impact on what work gets done and how it gets done.

However, instead of downsizing of reduction employees number aspect, it may also occur on other accepts, such as selling off, transferring out, merging businesses or altering the industry structure. It aims to improve organizational performance. Labeled workforce reduction strategies, focused mainly on eliminating headcount or reducing the number of employees in the workforce. It aims to early retirements, transfers and outplacement, by-out packages. This kind downsizing strategy whether it can bring performance improving benefit to organization or not in long term? Less employees work whether it will still improve performance, although the organization can reduce salary expenditure . Otherwise, if the organization does not reduce staffs number, it chooses to workforce reduction, work redesign and systemic strategies , whether it will be better than staffs number reduction strategy ?

What are critical success factors influence any organizations' strategic downsizing success implement ? Addresses the rationale utilized by firms to downsize, the expected outcomes in terms of economic and human consequences, and specific strategy. Also , downsizing tactics, human resources as assets to cost planning, participation, leadership, communications and support to victims . survivors are examined to any attempt implementing downsizing organizations.

In past organizations, when many blue-collor workers are also to trade off wage freezes for jobs security. White-dollars workers in the lower ranks of white-collar workers are often dismissed by downsizing, due to firms are increasingly forced to cut costs, restructure, and reduce their labor force. Instead of western countries firms are popular to accept downsizing . Downsizing has even become common in industrialized countries, such as Japan and Sweden, restructing in the 1990s led to employment reductions in industry and thus, increases in the levels of unemployment. Hence, downsizing may cause low ranks of white-collar workers feel job security lose in any time when they are working in any organizations, because white-collar workers are different to blue-collar workers have unions protection.

However, there are three perspectives from when downsizing can be reviewed : The industry level, the organization level and the individual level in terms of industry or global perspective, it may include , mergers, acquisitions, joint ventures, the organizational and strategy level may include how to implement downsizing and the expected bebefits of downsizing on the firm's performance, efficiency , and at the individual psychological level, it includes employee himself/herself stress, negative emotion feeling , due to he/she is dismissed. Hence, any organizations need to considerate how downsizing brings negative emotion to influence every dismissed employees. Because , their leave which will influence the continue working employee's emotion feel fear to be dismissed in next. If the present employees often feel stress to work, then their performance and efficiency will be influenced to worse. So, any organizations can not neglect to care the current working employees individual emotin in order to avoid low efficiency and poor performance to their organizations. Becaus every employee will have possible to be unreasonable dismiss, due to downsizing organizational influence.

On possible reason for this occurrence, is that firms poorly planned or carried out earlier downsizing projects and hence must remedy past facilities. So, one planned downsizing strategy will avoid negative emotion to influence current employees' works. But, factory workers will have possible to encounter dismiss , due to technological improvements, e.g. robotics can reduce to have additional workers rather than replacing the existing employees. So, when the factory begins to apply robotics , then employees number will be reduced. It is technological manufactuer causes downsizing to factory workers reason. It is due to raise productive efficiency factor , more than reducing cost reason to cause downsizing need to any organizations.

The term downsizing was first used reforcing to strategies to reduce personnal. However, it was become more and more relevant , its scope has been expanded and noe refers to a wide range of management measures towards better adopting on organizations to its environment (Gandolfi & Hanson, 2011).

reference

Gandolfi , F. & Hanson, M. (2011). Causes and consequences of downsizing : towards an integrative framwork, Journal of

management & organization , 17(4), 498-521.

In general, it is needed to implement strategies, due to the organization feels that without achieving the required organizational changes, this failing toobtain the desired results (Magan & Cespeses, 2012).

The downsizing methods may include: retrenchment specialized production, concentrating activities until economies of scale have been achieved. Downscaling strategy is toward again reducing in a smaller differentiation of activities in the value chain , it aims to keep the organization to reduce complexity in the organization. For some organizations had begun to implement robotic factory, because they expect that manufacturing robotics can help they to specialize production, raise productive efficiency. Hence, they only concentrate on keeping the proficient workers, they can cooperate to robotics to work in order to raise more products number efficietntly every day. So, the low skillful workers will be dismissed and they will re-employ the owning control manuacturing robotics skillful new workers to replace them. So, future manufacturing robotic manufacture plants causes downsize, it will be one good example for specialized production, concenating activities until economies of sale reasons to cause downsizing factory workers need to the owning manufacture robotics plant organizations. So, downsizing has an impact on raising productivities on specialized production and concentrating activities until economies of scale aim more than reducing cost to the owning manufacturing robotic factories organizations.

Thus, downsizing activities aim to improve organizational efficiency, productivity and/or competitiveness that affect the size of the firm's workforce, costs and the work processes. Downsizing may include: building-down , de-hiring, de-recruitment, reduction in force, re-sizing and right -sizing. So, in macroeconomic factors view, global competiton , technological innovations ,a change in business strategy retains competitive advantages may cause why some organizations decide to implement downsizing strategy.

However, one successful downsizing strategy implements to any organizations, organizations can not only consider themselves benefits, they also need to consider the psychological contract between employer and employee as new mutual expectations on workplace environment. Frequently described as re-organization, restructing, downsizing or real sizing, the human resource effects of these changes have often been very destructive to individual lives, employment relationships and organizational efficiency. If mployees recognized that their company was creative and consistent action to pressure their employment (security, trust could be reestablished and the success of the adoptive strategies. They can feel that their organizations decide to achieve the downsizing strategy is very reasonable more than unreasonable strategy in the right time. For example, when the organization decides to implement downsizing srategy before, they may enquire to their staffs opinions and acknowledge what their emotions, e.g. information on when change provided, staff views on the change are sought and are acted upon, staff have the opportunity to voice disagreement, support from manager during the change, to let they feel that change process seen as fair and equitable to let staff feel job security during the change process, and staff are trained to meet new job roles. So, all these factors may influence present employees have confidence to continue to work in your organizations after downsizing strategy is implemented. So, any organizations can not neglect to consider their present employees' feeling or emotion in order to avoid many staffs decide to leave their organizations after downsizing strategy in implemenation later.

reference
Magan , A. & Cespeses, J. (2012). Why are Spanish companies implementing downsizing. Review of business 32(2), 5-22.

● Business growth strategy

What factors cam affect the performance and growth to small businesses? Why and how obstacles are problematic for growth? How these differ between micro, small and medium sized businesses? How the obstacles are shaped?
Any businessmen had a substative growth ambition, but it can not represent that growth ambitin must sicceed to grow up their businesses. However, they must need to solve challenges when they expect grow their businesses successfully. The unpredicted external environment , include market changing and the vision of the owner and their attitudes towards growth will influence whether their businesses can grow up in success.
Hence, if the new business can keep negative growth, it ought may suceed. Some strategies , business owners need to consider that these factors will obstacle to their growth, such as during a recession, their businesses ought be difficult to growth, strategic planning is only useful when the business has a definit objective in mind, investment in research and development is too risky, expensive and difficult for a small business, there is no way,we can improve cashflow situation, factoring is only useful, if you ave in trouble, employees do not want formal, pay-related incentives and they are no use in helping business grow, we do not need to engage the staff in a structured, involving way, we can not get recruits to fit our needs, our business don't need to restructure our management as our business grow.
● How whether what obstacles can affect small business growth?
I assume small businesses have general staffs number with 50 or less than 50 staffs . Also, growth ambition was higher among younger business owners. The business owner personal poor time management factor may be one obstacles, for example, a lack of management time was rated to be the most difficult obstacle for potential exporters,

which is something of an obstacles for the significant exporters, little knowledge of how to export and difficulty in finding customers also attract higher ratings from potential exporters, e.g. the fear of payment problems, the cost of exporting and being too small to export are rated as being less significant obstacles by potential exporters and their perceptions are not to distant from the significant exporters. So, lack of management time and little knowledge of how to export may be the business ower's significant obstacles.

However, many small businesses are facing values number reducing challenges. How adoption to improve sale performance? Sale improvement strategy may include: appreciated new customers, more advertising, devised a new marketing strategy, dedicated sales/ marketing manager, undertaken training in marketing sales.

Overall, making this transition from being a micro business to a small business clearly requires a greater confidence in dealing with such matters, though, undertaking activity more frequently or simply the earger scale of the business necessitating increased familiarity and competence. Also, employing a professional manager can be seen as generally enabling a company to improve.

The aim of focus groups was to explore a company to improve owners' views on growth, including how they conceptialize growth, perceived barriers,the consequences of growth and personal cirsumstances and evidence of mindsets among owners which may restrict their potential business growth. In general, family owning-business strategies may include: maintain quality and higher prices, rather than lower prices raising the value added of products and shifting into a less marketplace and the emphasis towards areas where they sold direct to end clients, rather than acting as subsontractors, whose margins were being squeezed, up-selling in terms of volume or value to existing customers , e.g. a catering establishment noted then they tried to encourage customers to return, or an accountancy practice and a range of extra services.

Many owners did also acknowledge that the would likely more if they were more actively intending to grow business or if they saw evidence of potentially opportunities. Several those lacking a current plan were aware of a growing need to develop both a more strategies outlook and more formal systems, because of a general neglect of strategic thought, with a number noting that years of unplanned growth has left them realizing that the development of the busines, needed to catch up with the situation that they had found themselves in.

● What can impact on growth strategies on business?

Overall, making this transition from being a micro business to a small business clearly requires a greater confidence in dealing with such matters, through undertaking activity more frequently or simply the earger scale of the business necessitating measured familiarity and competence. Also, employing a professional manager can be seens as generally enabling a company to improve.

The aim of the focus groups was to explore in depth business owners' views on growth, including how they conceptualize growth, perceived barriers, the consequences of growth and personal circumstances and evidence of mindsets among owners which may restrict their potential business growth. In general, family ownin, business strategies may include: maintain quality and higher prices, rather than lower pruces raising the value added of products and shifting into a less marketplace and the emphasis towards areas where they sold direct to end clients, rather than acting as subcontractors, whose margins were bring squeezed, up-selling in terms of volume or value to existing customers , e.g. a catering establishment noted that they tried to encourage customers to return, or an accountancy practice and a range of extra services.

Manyowners did also acknowledge that they would likely plan more if they were more actively intending to grow business, or if they saw evidence of potentially opportunites. Several of those lacking a current plan were aware of a growing need to develop both a more strategic outlook and more formal systems, because of a general neglect of strategic thought, with a number noting that years of unplanned growth had left than realiaing that the development of the business needed to catch up with the situation that they had found themselves in.

● What can impact on growth strategies on business ?

Growth is important and key on survival of any business profit venture. Formulating and implementing effective growth strategies may enhance business pforit to any dynamic organization . Developing growth strategies to attract human resources, including increase in the sales volume per annum, an increase in the production capacity, increase in employment, increase in production volume and increase in the all of material, increase energy and power, these factors may influence the business's strategy is implemented effectively in order to achieve growth aim.

Growth strategies that a business enterprise may wish to adopt include: understanding customer expectation, service, positioning, market segementation, setting measuring market standards, relationship marketing, human resource strategy and successful communication strategy these factors may influence business growth success. When one organization ensures that it can achieve growth, it may evaluate to measure its overall performance by these several aspects, they may include sales, assets base, employee retention goodwill and increase business profits that drive investment and economic development. Business growth may introduce new products and services, or adding new features to existing products. Growth could also mean expansion of an organization in order to buy new assets develop new products or service to enhance new investments in the economy. I shall refer some growth strategies as below:

Market penetration strategy focuses on expanding sales of a company's existing products or services in an existing market. It may attract new customer for the products and increase the usage or purchase rate of existing customers , it is often achieved by increasing activities through more intensive distribution and competitive pricing promotion.

Market expansion or market development means to move it into a completely new market. This strategy is about existing product which are offered in a new market when a region business wants to expand, or when new markets are opening up, or new use is found for the existing product.

Product expansion or product development strategy means introducing a new idea into a company's existing market. It offers new products to an existing market. It tried to grow by developing improved products for the present market. Diversification means companies with sell new products or new market. It is very risky strategy . It needs to research market to determine if consumers in the new market will potentiallu like the new products. Acquisition means the purchase of one company by another company. It may be private or public.

The new growth strategy can be used as an alternative channel. It involves pursuring cutomers in different ways for instance selling a company's products or services online . Through the use of the internet a customer can access products or services of a particular company in a new (alternative). It goes beyond envisioning a long-term success. It has to be follow these steps: establishing a value for the company, identifying an ideal customer , who is loyal to the company, defining a company's key indicators, verifying revenue streams for cost reduction, seeking competition in the external environment, focusing on company's strength (internal), investing in talents (effective human resources who are creative and innovation). So, managers must achieve on growth strategy to enable stakeholders not only to plan, but also to track organic growth in their revenue and allow effective and efficient allocation of resources toward a more centered effort to adapt to frequent changes in the company and the industry occasioned by technology and the differences in competition.

Hence, of growth strategies are effectively formulated and implemented according to indicators and plan, it will lead to increase a profit in that organization . Growth strategies are often called the master business strategies, they provide the basic direction for strategies action. They are the coodinated and efforts indirected towards achieving long term business objectives and profit. Growth strategies have played central roles in the expansion and profit. They have enabled organizations to increase market shares, develop new markets, and develop new products and services, so business profit will continue to increase economic development.

● Why and how can organizational life cycle models influence organizational performance?

What does organizational life cycle mean? Must any organizations have life cycle? What do the influences when the organization reachs the organizational life cycle stage? Can the organization implement any useful strategy , if had ability to known whether what stage is its organizational life cycle? I shall explain as below:

In general, organizational life cycle has three stages: Birth, young, and maturity or decline. The related goals of profit, growth and survival seem to have overall goal structures of most organizations. IN general, most organizations will experience all three stages. However, not all organizations pass through all three stages. In fact, only about one-half of all new busness, organizations survive longer than one and half years. Relatively few for profit or not -for-profit organizations survive long time to experience all three stages. I assume that profits growth is one main factor to influence any organizations whether it can experience long whole three stages in their organizational life cycle.

What is the three stages chacracteristics of organizational life cycle? In birth stage, a merger or a point venture may occasionally lead to the creation of a new organization. A organization may be either a single person expands or an entrepreneur cooperates people to help promote a new idea, product or service. The motive in both cases is usually the desire for profit. In youth stage, when professional management is taken over by a family with a controlling interest, the organization's primary goal often changing from profit to growth. The new management team wants to demonstrate its competence and growth is the most obvious aim. For example, a manager of a large organization must consider how much company's return an investment in the organization's growth stage in this new growth stage. It has these characteristics: goals become less specific, less measurable, increasing emphasis on marketing, hoping for the increases sales that will justify the expansion of plant anf acquisition of new, more effecticient tools and equipment. Finally in the maturity / decline stage, as an organization matures and starts to decline, a desire to survive which will be the organization's goal in this stage. Why does organization may experience this stage, the organization can evaluate whether it is experiencing this stage, depends on these factors, e.g. when organization increases large , its technology is complex, its structure is bureaucratic, it is financially oriented, it is greatly affected by market and social forces and it is so complex when it grows up its organization, it will increases more new departments and it will employ many extra staffs and it will create many new positions. Hence, it explains why the organization can survive long time, and it can experience all three stages, it must be more succefful to compare the another organization can not experience all three stages , because it is common that when the organization can experience all three stages. It must survive long time. Also, it means that it can earn profit growth . Otherwise, when the organization can only experience birth stage or youth stage , then it can not survive long time and without profit growth in possible.

Hence, when one organization can experience all three stages. It may be one successful profit growth organization, e.g. although one sale trade earn less profit, and its organization size is small, but the jobb trader's business can survive a long time. So, he/she sole trading organization may experience birth, young, and mature or decline stages. So, organizational life cycle model can be applied to large or middle or small size organization, even sale trader, partnership organization to help them to evaluate whether their businesses are experiencing which stage in order to implement the most suitable or reasonable strategies to help them to solve present challenges more easily.

● What is the essential elements of life cycle model to assist business development ?

Although, when one organization feels it encoounters the decline stage, it means that its organization has possible that it can not continue survive. But if it has good strategy to help itself to solve present challenges. It has chance to renew or continue to develop its business functions to be better. Then, it has chance to continue survive. Usually, when the business is experiencing decline stage, it ought decide to change its business direction in order to continue survue . For example, raising its capabilities of organizational learning and innovations, creating new profitable and vision into the renew survival stage, and increasing its competitiveness in cost. However, the decline stage is characteristics by deterriorating profits and a loss of market share. The renewing firms have a rebuild their learning and innovative capabilities and shape a new profit direction for business. The contribution links interactions of development more effective business functions to provide a tool to help the experiencing decline stage organizations to learn how to implement new strategies to solve their present challenges in order to continue survive.

Hence, what is the essential elements to help the experiencing decline stage organizations to have possible to continut survive. I shall explain as below: In old economic society, manufacturing firms whose main driver to standardize production, products and busines processes. By constrast, the new economic society, we are experiencing information business, utilize information to differentiate, personalize and dispatch over networks at an rapid speed, small as e-commerce. It is obvious tht old economy's traditional shop business model is not popular to be accepted by consumers. Consumer shopping behaviors have been changed to choose online shopping to replace visiting shops shopping behavior. So, it seems that why some businesses will experience decline stage within one year. It is possible that their traditional business visiting step shopping method is not popular to be accept to themselves businesses, it is right time.

They need to design website store to let customers can choose online shopping when they visit themselves website stores from internet. So, e-commerce can influence some businesses to experience the decline stage in short time rapidly. It may be one factor to influence any organizational life cycle stge to be shorten in short time. It is one technological innovation element to shorten any organization's life cycle in short time. So, any businessmen ought not neglect technological innovation new influence their businesses development as well as they need to continue pursue their new sale method direction, e.g. payment by smartphone shopping method, electronic commerce payment transaction payment method, in order to keep high technological or payment channel to attract customers. The another element is how to deliver customer focused to feel differentiation, to fight for survival in the global market, a company needs to implement innovation function to cope effectively with the changes in the customers' needs. So, it is innovation element to the experiencing decline stage organization to help it to attempt to solve challenges in order to continue survive in possible . Innovation may include service, e.g. sale service, client service, delivery service etc. as well as product innovation ,e g. design change to the cup, mobile technological improvement, car style, design, engine, chargeable battery charge etc. or individual innovation, e.g. the fundamental assumption of operate culture changes, mindset of the top manger, CEO midset change and questioned by the capability of execution of the operations function to himself organization. How to innovate organizational learning, whether and what experience or knowledge applied in the operations function can be executed for the next innovation in order to renew the experiencing decline stage organization strategy to continue survive. So, innoviation is also one element to influence organization's survival.

● What can learn from the organizational life cycle theory?

The next element is whether organization can continue keep on learning element. In fact, there are many different factors to influence whether our organizational survival. They may include organizational internal factors as well as outside factors. In general organizations can control themselves internal to be better, but they can not control outside environment, because they can not predict when environments, e.g. economic environment, customer shopping desires, when new competitors enter market. According to organizational life cycle theory, during the firm's growth from inception to high growth, to maturity firm characteristics differ and the internal resources and capabilities of the firm develop.

Organizations encounter an unpredictable business environment which is constantly pressured by the changing effects of globalization , competition and technological advancement within the context of the knowledge economy (Thoumrungroje & Tansuhaj, 2007).

reference

Thoumrungroje, A. & Tansuhaj, P. (2007). Globalization effects and firm

perferences. Jounral of international business research, 6 (2),43-58.

During the first stage, any organization will up in a new business environment with much adaptation and try to develop a niche through, learning and innovative practices. Given the success of that survival, the organization becomes aggressive in the second stage in how to managing internal resources, effectiveness and efficiency, learning workflows, and corporate structure to accommodate the increased complexity of operations, policies are needed to implement in second stage. The third stage, business efficiency is the core, and the organization keeps resolving workplace problems and defining clear objectives of what to achieve short and long term in the business. In this stage, revenue is the key pursue aim or objective. The final stage, as a nature stge, the organization tends to maintain the business stability and spend time focusing on the status of how organizational structure, management departments cooperation strategy implementation and organizational culture in order to help the organization itself and the CEO leader himself/herself how to manage her/his organization successfully . So, whether the organization can continue keep on learning , it may be one important element to influence the organization to develop in business.

● How to develop organizations in growth stage?

Theoretical development of the organization life cycle has description of distinct stages of organization growth, Little attention to the dynamics of organization growth, such as how to grow the organization? Why can the organization grow rapidly ? I believe any organizations expect that they can grow rapidly, but the organizations expect that they can grow rapidly, but the question concens: What factors influence the organization can not grow rapidly, e.g. lacking proficient staffs, lacking high technological manufacture, lacking creating mindset or innovation, lacking suitable strategy implementation, strong new competitors enter, customers taste change etc. different organizational internal and external environment etc. factors. So, any organizations expect to grow rapidly, they need to solve the challenges to threaten their grow. For example, one mobile manufacturer only concentrates on manufacturing new technological smart phones products . So, at this stge, it ought pursue a niche strategy, presenting a very narrow smart phone product time, often a single smart phone product to a single smart phone user market. The new different design and function of smart phone products venture generally undertakes major and frequent smart phone product innovation. Major investments are needed to make in smart phone products development, robotic plant and manufacture robotic equipment is needed. So, this smart phone product manufacture firm expects to grow its smart phone share market rapidly. It must often need to innovate itself manufacturing technology , e.g. manufacturing robotics as well as designers need have good creative mindset to attempt to design any kinds of smart phones and change kind functions and smart phone design in ordeer to satisfy smart phone users' needs. When , it often have different kinds of new smart phone products design. I believe that it can grow itself smart phone productive speed rapidly, when it can attract many smart phone users to choose its any kinds of smart phone products to buy to use in preference . Hence, this smart phone manufacturing firm needs have good design mindset to attract smart phone consumers' attention if it expects to reach the growth stage in short time. If it feels that it has not increase smart phone customer number significant in this time, it may believe that its busines can not reach growth stage in the moment. Hence, the life cycle theory offers expected obstacles for each stage, which can help the firms to solve the problems and help them to attempt to find any useful strategies accordinglyly.

Hence, organizational life cycle can help any organizations to revise whether what obstacles can influence or threaten the organization itself can not grow easily, due to consumers demand have become more complex, as well as arket trends are harder to predict and competition is severe than ever, in order to survive companies, shoulf need to learn how to reach growth stage rapidly in order to raise its competitive ability to reach mature stage rapidly in short time. Becuase of the organization can reach mature stage from birth to young stage in short time rapidly. Then , it will have enough ability to avoid to reach decline stage rapidly. If it expects to continue survive or it does not need to review its organizational strategy ocnsequently. Because different stage, it will have different kinds of challenges to the organization will encounter, e.g. in the birth stage , challenges may include lacking cash flow, less customer number, without building attractive or famous product brand or image, in the young stage challenges, may include strategy is not suitable to implement effectively, customer growth speed is slow, product development or promotion challenges when the organization reachs mature stage, its challenges may include clients number begins decrease or loss old clients, product sale number begins reduction from the top level, customers feel its products are not attractive and they begin to choose to buy other similar feature of products to replace its products in market. Hence, when the organization can know whether it reachs which stage in its organizational life cycle model. Then, it may attempt to find the most suitable or the most reasonable strategy to implement in order to keep its long survival to stay on the mature stage more easily.

CHAPTER II

● Economic recession or boom how influences consumer behavior

COVID -19 disease how influence businesses may experience either growing life cycle stage or decline life cycle stage.

Nowadays, we are facing global economic recession period, since COVID 19 human mouth disease effect can bring economic crisis. Can it influence businesses feel difficult to adapt how global economic recession change after their decline life cycle stage? However, the effects of COVID 19 spreading will have wider implication , not just on how economies function, but also on how consumers behave, across china, Asia-pacific and around the world. Another effect of China;s economic rise is its influence in the adoption and adaption to new technological invention to manufacture , e.g. manufacturing robotic products had sold to China factories to replace workers to manufacturer products. It also will influence many China manufacturing workers lose jobs, when many China factories apply manufacture robotics to replace them in nowadays economic recession period.

Considering the adoption of online-offline shopping and home online office tasks, they are influenced by COVID-19 human disease influence, it also influences on regional travel in China, even global travel income is also reducing, because many travelers feel afraid to catch air planes to avoid to get COVID 19 human disease when they are sitting in close window airplanes by air . HOwever, COVID 19 also influences global consumer behavior changes to online shopping, because many people are afraid to enter crowd shops to avoid get COVID 19 human disease easily. So global shops will lose many visiting shop consumers, if they do not decide to attempt to open online stores to let customers to apply internet to buy their products. So, COVID 19 human mouth disease induced changes in consumer behavior. Shop online will be one new trend to influence young and old consumers make shopping from online stores. They will enquire whether the kind of product is worth to choose to buy by social media, e.g. facebook, online post . Hence, COVID19 human mouth disease may influence global economic recession, but it also brings e-commerce boom chance, when many consumers are fear to enter any crowd shops , when they need to stay long time in any shops. Then, they get COVID 19 human mouth disease chance will increase. Hence, it will influence many customers reduce to visit shops times, but it also creates online-shopping new business model . For example, China families are renewing their joy in home cooking. Onlins cooking videos are helping with the discovery od new recipes, new ways to create dishes , and new influences. So, opportunities are opening for more cleaning products, new ways to clean and new home hacks from online videos will bring global home consumers spend more time on their wellness or beauty routines ? So, COVID-19 disease also influences many families choose to cook dinner at homes at nght. Restaurants will lose many eating clients, because they are fear to enter restaurants to eat together to avoid to get COVID19 human mouth disease. But, it also creates home cooking products sale chance, e.g. rice cookers, dishes or any cooking tools because many families choose to cool at home. Hence, in some situation, economic recession will create new business chance , such as online store or rice cooker sale increases, they may be influenced in this COVID 19 human mouth disease occurrence environment.

Economic recession also influences business strategy changes. Many companies seem to be applying many aspects of a retrenchment approach , e.g. reduced fixed costs, narrower product offering, reduced staffs, but also there are some aspects of an investment approach which can be observed , because customers number will be influenced to reduce in economic recession environment. Companies have felt the robustness and quality of the approaches being applied had been allowed to decline. As a consequence of the challenges of a recession, urgent improvement have needed to be made because factories will reduce workers number to avoid salary expenditure spending more , but customers umber reduced in recession environment .

Hence, they will choose to buy manufacturing robotics to replace workers. If robotics can be improved to be proficient manufacture. Then, they won't need to buy many robotics to help them to replace to replace many workers to manufacture any products efficiently. So, manufacturing and improvement to robotics number demand may increase to any factories , e.g. vehicle manufacture, electronic products, e.g. computer hime cooking electronic products , e.g. rice cookers, heaters etc. products may be manufactured by manufacturing robotics. It creates the manufacturing robotic sale improvement quality chance in recession environment. It may impact on medium, or long term, it depends on how long time of recession. So, economic recession may bring robotic manufacture industry boom , when electronic products manufacturers need many improved robotics to replace workers in factries in order to reduce spending too much salaries expenditure in recession.

It is one external environmental factor to influence sudden manufacture robotic industry boom absolutely ,because electronic manufacturer's manufacturing robotic needs increases in recession environment. So, robotic manufacturers' strategy need to change , such as how to improve any manufacturers' needs in recession, e.g. manufacturing robotic product categories, market segments, geographic areas, core technologies, reliability , price, customisation, robotic manufacturing efficiency how to be improved of business.Change strategy to any manufacturing robotics manufacturers. So, recession may influence some kinds of manufacturing robotics' needs raise in robotic manufacturing market.

● How recession influences the role of advertising changes?

Advertising plays a key role in a dynamic economy. It may provide valuable information about products and services in an efficient manner, communicates client value, builds brand awareness and creates demand. However, when one country is experiencing recession, how it influences the country's businessmen spending on advertisement behaviors? Due to clients number reduces, a company usualy cuts come from the advertising budget than companies begin to cut back on advertiseing during an economic recession, they become less visible to the public because they predict clients number ought reduce next three months, even half year or one year. It depends on how long economt recession occurs. So, economic recession many impact any companies' advertising budget expenditure to be reduce . How much on the reduction on advertising budget expenditure, it depends on the company predicts how many clients number will reduce.However, due to advertising number reduces, it can influence consumer behavior changes indirectly.

In economic boom environment, consumers can watch to different kinds advertisement from television. Advertisement may bring positive alternative evaluation phase of biying decision-making process is bring exposed to buy several communication messages. In such an economic boom environment, any organizations may be clearly heard by the consumers, after any advertisement programs are broadcasted on television. Therefore, advertisemtn can persuade clients to choose to buy the kind of product after the kind of product advertisement is broadcasted from television absolutely.

However, when recession occurs, any companies; advertisement time is shortened , even number is reduced . Hence, they can not receive any client's positive or negative feedback immediately in short time afer advertisements are broadcasted from television . So, recession may influence advertisement time is shortened and number is rediced . On consequence, companies can not have any repsonse to know whether how market or customers' demand is changing to themselves products in shor time.

However, recession may bring worse advertisement effect to influence any businesses . On one hand, there is a negative economic recession environment because of the negative media reporting, these would be a decline in demand for the products and services and eventually companies would want to save more than they spend , But in the other hand, when the companies cut back advertiseing expenditures, they become less visible to public. Hence recession may influence many companies brand image will be lost, due to spending on advertisement expenditure wil reduce. Then, clients number may be influenced to reduce, because they can not watch the kind of product advertment from television home often.

When one country is encountering recession, how are the various components of household consumption affected ? How is the impact of the recesion distributed across socio-demographic group? How does the recession compare to previous recessions? When book will boom? In fact, any country's recession may impact consumer behavior changes, it depends on these factors: age, race, education and wealth groups resulted in a decline in consumption inequality. The rich group is the " wealth effect influence group" when recession comes, it may influence their wealth reduces, so their enjoyment dsires will be influenced to reduce, e.g. purchase expensive cars driving enjoyment desires, purchase expensive house living enjoyment desires. If one rich person loses jobs , it may influence him to spend less time to drive themselves cars, so consumption of gasline will be influenced to reduce.

Economic theory (e.g. consumer behavioral economic theory) predicts that when economic recession occurs, it will cause many businesses may experience decline cycle life stage rapidly, that link between income shocks and consumption has close relationship, such as rich person consumer group, if his income reduces, then he will buy less gas to drive himself car, even if he loses his job in recession environment, he will choose to sell his car to exchange cash. Hence, consumption may fall as a direct consequence of a fall in income induced by job loss, reduced hours or productivity and negative returns from assets, if there are long term changes to a household's econmic resource in recession environment. Hence, in recession environment, job loss or income reduction factors that may affect consumers and their shopping attitudes in the recession period. Otherwise, for low income group, recession may influence food consumption to low income consumer behavior changes to worse. Because low income person may reduce income ot lose job, then cheap food consumption will be influenced to worse to low income consumer group. In recession period, if the food price is raised , due to the cost increase of food, it will lead to change in the reductin on quantity and type of food being purchase to low income food buyers. This may lead to a reduction in the quantity of food consumed and/or the substitution of high-priced food for cheaper food, which is often less nutritous and of worse quality. Hence in recession perios, low income food consumers will consider whether the kind of food price has how much increase or decrease. They won't consider the quantity of food consumed for maintaining energy balance and the quality of food consumed for maintaining ample intakes of protains, fats and micronutrients, such as vitamins, minerals and trace elements on food issue. So, if the kind of food price reduced in recession period, it ought may attract many low income food consumers number, even its food nutritious is worse. Hence, if the kind of meat price can be reduced in recession , the cheap types of meat consumption to low income consumer may be increased, even its nutritious is worse to compare the recession occurs before period.

On conclusion, in either economic recession or boom period, in general, consumer behavior will be influenced to change. Some products may be influenced to have higher sale in recession period, e.g. home electronic rice cookers , due to COVID 19 human mouth disease influenced many households choose to cook dinner at home at ight. Otherwise, some products may be influenced to have lowr sale., e.g. expensive cars sale in recession period, many high income people may lose jobs or reduce salaries , then it will influence their car purchase desires to be reduced. But if COVID 19 human mouth disease has medicine to kill this kind of disease. Then, economy will boom, many households will choose to go to restaurants to eat dinner. The, the electronic rice cookers sale number may reduce, when they reduce time to cook at home at night. Hence, it explains why economic recession or boom period may have impact to influence consumer behavior in behavioral economic view.

Applying business development strategy to raise the educational robotic manufacturer sale number in recession period

● What does business development strategy ?

An effecting business development strategy ought have these five steps: The first step is market analysis. Who are your clients , knowledge of your market? Second step is how to adopt for each penetration, your business needs to learn how to adopt for each group of clients, your first need to review your own capacbility. It is important that you are realistic and honest with yourselves over where clients truly sit, learn how to classify your clients into similar groups relative is the scale of the opportunity. Third step learns how to review your performance , market matrix to plot your results to help you determine your market penerstion. In addition, it will help you then discuss and consider various strategies for growth. By potting your clients you will get a sense of where your strengths and weaknesses are against the opportunity that total market offer.Fourth step learns how to consider alternative growth strategies on the market matrix. The final step , you need to consider these questions in order to decide whic is the most effective strategy for your business. For example, which model is the most (least effective? Why? which model work best for line managers, HR are finance, why? How might we most effectively progress from one model to the most reasonable questions?) Then, you will need to decide how to launch new services, new products, opening new markets, how accessing new geographic territories.

● How to apply business development strategy to help educational robotic manufacturers to enter traditional education market ?

Many thinkers concern robots that are used in manufacturing workplaces, homes, roads, hospitals and care centre aspect, but they don't feel robotics may be possible to apply on social service aspect, e.g. educational service aspect . In fact, robotic may have both functions. Industrial robotics, e.g. manufacturing function as well as service robotics, e.g. professional robotcs, medical robotics, entertainment robotics, e.g. toy and education robotics and service robotics , e.g. personal and domestic robotics.

Educational robotic is on the birth stage in its industry life cycle. So, any educational robotic products will need time to persuade schools or any educational institutions to buy their products to assist teachers to teach students in classrooms. The question is how to apply business development strategy to help the educational robotic manufacturer to develop its educational robotic products to persuade educational clients to choose to buy ? I shall attempt to explain as below:

Due to educational robotic product is one new educational tool to assist any schools to buy to assist teachers to improve teaching service performance to let students to feel more learning satisfaction, so any educational robotic products must need time to introduce whether what it can bring schools benefits to let students and teachers to feel. When robotic can be popular to use on manufacturing, educational service industries aspect, e.g. warehouse , factory, shopping center, even restaurant's kitchen cooking robotics, office environment's accounting, law draft etc. clerical robotics may be invented to replace human 's general simple tasks. However, if future robots can be applied to educational aspect, e.g. classroom, school teaching students. Can educational robotic may assist or replace teachers to teach students in clasrooms? Will future teachers be replaced by teaching robotics . I shall attempt to explain whether it is possible that educational robotic can be developed to global educational organizations successfully as below:

Robotic technology has been invented to own " mind " ability, e.g. writing words, writing song, simple calculation tasks reading tasks . So, future robotics can be invented to own " mind " ability, when robotics' mind ability can be improved to own how to " communication" ability and " analytical" ability. Then can it be possible to apply robotics to do teaching tasks in classrooms, e.g. learning any books , the it applies the book's contents to analyze any "knowledge" in order to follow the logic mind to teach students in classroom. It is one major factor to influence any schools to explain why they need to buy any educational robotic in schools in any educational robotic product business development strategy. So, they need to find whether what their educational robotic strengths , any competitors won't own or their product weaknesses, they need to improve their educational robotic products in order to attract educational organizations to choose to buy.

Can future teaching robotics learn to do teacher individual same education tasks? It will be absolute competitive point to any educational robotic product manufactures. If it is true, can teaching robotics may be trained to exceed teacher individual teaching skill? It is another competitive point to any educational robotic product manfacturers. Is it ethic to apply robotic to teach students to replace teachers if teaching robotic can perform better teaching service to compare teachers? If the eduational robotic manufactuer can persude the school can accept eduational robotic ethic issue to assist or replace teachers to do teaching tasks, then it's sale chance will raise. So, ethic to educational robotic will be another factor to develop the educational robotic business. Can teachers be teaching robotic's teaching assistant role if teaching robotics can have teaching ability to teacher in the school? So, if the educational robotic manufacturer can persuade the school to feel that its products can be teacher's assistant to improve their performance to let students learn more easily. The educational robotics manufacturer may develop its product to sell in this educational market more easily, in business development strategy view.

All of these will be future any one educational robotic development challenges if they hope their products can sell more easily. They also need to know to let schools to know these disadvatages to their products to become advatanges in order to attract they to choose to buy their producte more easily. Such as what potential harmful consequences may come from the inventing of teaching robotics? What happends to important education moral, such as teacher or school privacy then robotic are starting to become an teaching tool to the school? Do such robotics hace any roght and responsibilities if the class has many students learning ability are influenced to poor or examination results are poor when the educational robotic has been bought to assist the school teachers to teach their students? Why does the school need to buy educational robotic to do teaching tasks? Any school organizations must need any one educational robotic product seller to answer any one of above questions, before they decide to buy their products.

So, they must need to ensure teaching robotics will be used to help the school to teach students to learn more understanding to compare teachers only.

● Future educational robotic are applied on development teaching maths market

In the future, business development to educational robotic market may be teaching maths. I shall explain as below:

It is possible that students can use mobile robotic to learn mathematics subject to compare teachers more easily. Why? For example, young age from 4 to 14 age, they may apply mobile robotics to learn add, multiple, divided, simple math equation more understanding than math teaches. Robotic kints and apps is currently available on the maket for teacher of 4 to 14 age students,due to mobile , kits app price is cheap. So, they can be popular to be accepted by any primary schools , even in secondary schools, robotics may be applied to teach computer science, statistical methods subjects of one robotic kit for teach team of 2 to 3 students, short theory lessons , and tutorials to link theory and practice, realistic but affordable tasks linked with curricular subjects, teachers at ease with the robotic etc. So, future primary and secondary , even university teachers may need to choose the more suitable robot kit for their students,and carefully design where and how to use it and with which role.In fact, children will be possible to raise interest to learn when they can contact for any kind of teaching robotic to learn maths in classrooms together. So, teaching robotics may help 4 to 14 children students to raise learning interest instead of learning about ability.

In the future, robotic role is school may be one tool to engage the students as teachers role may be transfer base knowledge when teachers teach maths, geography, statistics, computer science subjects to promary , secondary even university students. This is one good example , whether what subjects robotic may be applied when it is invented to own human mind and anlaytical skill and communication ability. Robotics can perform more better to be applied to teach these subjects. It can let students to understand easily, e.g. understanding how to create equations that describe numbers a relationship understanding solving equations as a process of reasoning and explain the equations and inequalities in one variable, helping students to find different solutions, then best solves the problem , given the criteria and the constraints, helping students have more understanding how science knowledge is based upon logical and conceptual connections between evidence and explanations, even robotc can ask questions that can be investigated within the scope of the classroom, outdoor environment, and museums and other public faciltities with available resources and when appropriate frame a hypothesis based on observation and scientific principles. Even, robotics may help students to learn how construct, use and present oral and written arguments supported by evidence and scientific reasoning to support or refute an explanation or a model for a phenomenon, or robot can hep students to learn how obtain, evaluate and communicate information in 6-8 builds on k-5 and progresses to evaluating the merit and validity of ideas and methods, integiate qualitative scientific and technical information in written text with that contained in media and visual displays to clarify cliams and findings, helping students to anlyze data from texts to determine similarities and differences among several design solutions to identify the best characteristics of each that can be combined into a new solution to better meet the criteria for success, even helping students to learn how analyze data in 9-12 builds on k-8 and progresses to introducing more detailed statistical anslysis, the comparision of data sets for consistency and the use of models to generate and analyze data, analyze data using tools, technologies , and/or models e.g. computational, mathematical in order to make valid and variable scientific claims or determine and optinal design solution more easily than human teacher. So, there are human-made educaton machine advantage to students more than human teacher.

Educational robotic has been introduced as a powerful, in fact, flexible teaching / learning tool stimulating learns to control the behavior of tangible model using specific programming languages (graphical, or textual and involving them actively in authentic problem -solving activities. Howeverm in future educational robotic development, it may be divided two separate categories as below:

Robotics as learning object: This first category includes educational activities where robotics is being studied as a subject on its own. It includes educational activities aimed at configuring a learning environment that will actively involve learners in the solution of authentic problems, facing on robotics -related subjects, such as robot construction, robot programming and artificial intelligence as well as robotic as learning tool: In the frame of this second category, robotics is proposed as a tool for teaching and learning other school subjects at different school levels. Robotics as learning tool is usually, seen as an interdisciplinary, project -based learning activity drawing mostly on science, maths, informatics and technology and offering major new benefits to education in genera at all levels. However, I believe the role of teacher is crucial for the successful industry of technological and innovations in classrooms, when robotics are been particiapted to any education tasks in classrooms. Schools can focuse on the training of prospective and in-service teachers in the use of robotics technologies through courses.

In future electronic learning environment, robotics can be participated, such as recognised their active participation in all sessions of the course and their creative involvement even in the theoretical parts introducing principles and methodology for designing robotic-enhanced projects, very much liked the activity-orientation of the educational content, acknowledged the central role of the e-workspace during the face-to-face meetings and beyond ehem in enhancing sense of community, acknowledged the potential of educational robotics as a teaching tool but also as a subject, in different disiplines , such as technology, informatics and engineerinfg, highly appreciated the opportunity to create their projects.

How to develop robotic in technological subjects on teaching, learning and educational aspect? Learners can be encouaged hen robotics participate actively in the learning process. Through robotic learners build something on their own, preferably a tangible object, that they can both touch and find meaningful. In robotic learners are invited to work experiments or problem-solving with selective use of available resources, according to their own interest, search and learning strategies. Robotics can help them to seek solutions to real world problems, based on a technological framework meant to engage students' movitation. So, when students can have control of specific robotc in a rich learning environment, the construction of robots and programs to control them the emphasis might move on interesting learning actiities in the frame of specific learning areas , such as science and technology. Thus, the design of robotic construction activities is associated with the fulfillment of a project aimed at solving a problem. In such a learning environment, learning is driven by the problem to be solved. To engage students in activities requiring to design and manufacture real objects, i.e. robotic structures that make sense for themselves and should devise activities that will encourage students to support in order experiment. So, robotic participation any science experiments, they may encourage students to create problem solving and combining interdisiplinary concepts from different knowledge areas,: science, mathematics , technology and research educational tasks, the role of students will change, when preparing a work with a programmable robotics studies experiment with simple programmable sobotics devices , e.g. a car-robot, motors, sensor etc. Students are asked to synthesize their finds and reach conclusions and solutions to the problem uner investigation. SO, robotic is educaional participation to any scientfic technological or research experiments, they may help students to work with creativity , imagination and independence and finally organize the evaluation of the activity in collaboration ith studens. Also robotic participation to any technological or scientific research experiemtn, it also change teacher role . The teacher is such a constructist theoretical framework, like that teacher 's role that does not transfer ready knowledge to students, but rather acts as a organizer, coordinator and facilitator of learning for students. when educational robotics participate to any science or technological any research experiments, students may be organize the learning environment, raise the question , problem to be solved by students allow students to work with creativity, imagination and independence and finally organize the evaluation of the activity in collaboration with students. So, any educational robotic manufacturers must let their school clients to feel all these benefits which can bring to let students to raise learning abilty and learning interest to compare that are only taught by teachers, if they hope their educational robotics can be sold successfully in business development strategy view.

CHAPTER III

Learning behavioral economy to solve social challenges

● Why do some social challenges may influence customers number ?

In our societies , we shall have different challenges to our every day. However, in general , the challanges seem that they do not have relate to influence businessmen profit, but in fact, these social challenges have relationship to influence business profit and clients number. I shall indicate some social challenges to explain why these social challenges may influence any business profit indirectly as below:

In investment or raving individual preference decision aspect, for some people , it may be interesting or fun to think cbout the best investments or the right health care plan. But, for other people, these choices are unpleasant, they may be persuaded to buy anythings, e.g. car, computer. So, if car seller can have persuasive methods to influence many people feel the health care plan or investment plan is not prefereable choices, driving car enjoyable feeling or material enjoyment is the most preference choice. Then I believe that the car seller's car selling number may increase, because some people greatly enjoy thinking about their pension and the best investment or health care insurance preferable decision, their decision had been influenced to choose to buy the car seller's cars. When they feel driving car enjoyable feeling is more important than future benefit.

Hence, in behavioral economy view, they had felt the driving car benefit is much to compare pension investment or health care insurance future benefit. The question is how to car seller can persuade these investment ot pension plan or health care preference decision individual to change purchase car driving decision>

I suggest that the car seller may have discount or cash coupon or installment payment method to attract them to consider , instead of advertisement promotion method. because this preference investment or pension saving or health care plan decision individual customer group will be more difficult to persuade them to choose to buy car immediately at this moment. Hence, if the car seller can not implement cheap car discount strategy, it will be difficult to attract this prefeence long term future benefit consumer to make purchase ca r decision easily. Because they think pension or investment or health care plan ce help them to bring long term future benefit, also it means that purchase car may only bring short term present benefit. It is general social behavioral consumption model to influence their purchase choice. Hence, I assume that general social long term future benefit product or service, e.g. insurance, investment , pension may influence th scocial shor tterm present benefit product , e.g. car consumer. It is the main reason, it can explain why car sellers can not persuade this long term future benefit consumers to make decision to buy their cars easily, when they have no enough money to spend to buy car and make investment, saving , medical care insurance , pension plan in the same time. They must need to make either purchase car or insurance etc. decision in our nowadays societies.

So, in behavioral economic view, it explains why consumer individual purchase choice behavior has relationship to himself/herself spending budget. I assume that it has two kinds of behavioral economic consumers. One kind if long term future economic benefit in preference more than short term present economic benefit, such as purchase car and investment or health care plan insurace saving term present benefit consumer, he / she considers to earn driving enjoyment at this moment is not preference than purchase insurance or investment future benefit decision . So, our society, any business will encounter these two kinds of behavioral consumer. They persuade either long term futuer benefit consumers or short term present benefit consumer to change himself/herself products or services more easily. Otherwise, such as if car seller can not implement coupon or cash reward or discount or installment cash payment strategy to attracr the long term future benefit consumer. Then, it will lose this group car customers number absolutely. So, it explains why businessmen need to learn consumer behavioral consumption model in order to increase client number more easily.

" Social welfare" usually measured by people's prefences, and it also focuses for the conventional economists, on how to maximize social welfare. What then is the task of behavior law and economics? Such as, this cate seller case example, whether what social welfare the car seller can bring to society when the individual decides to buy its car to drive or when the individual chooses to buy health care insurance or pension plan or investment . When he/she chooses to buy health care insurance or make pension plan or buys any companies' shares. Then, these investment service companies will bring what benefits to our society? So, instead of consumer benefit, we also need to consider whether the kind of product or service will bring what long term social benefit . However, I think that when global many people own cars, then many cars are driven on the roads, it will bring serious air pollution to influence our health. Then, when many people are got lung diseases by air pollution. Then, many people will need to pay more medical expense. It will be long term negative medical cost increasing expense to future us, but it also bring possible income for insurance firms, when many people plan to buy medical care plans when they feel air pollution will influence them to need to pay future medical expense. So, it seems that the effect on many people own cars and their driving behaviors will bring serious air pollution, but it will also create the health care medical insurance need to be increased due to many people feel air polluton will bring lung disease and they need to pay long time medical expensein the future long time in possible. So, many people driving behavior may bring air pollution, but it also bring medical insurance need increases in our society in possible. It means that air pollution may create medical insurance market develops in possible, such as most smokers say they would prefer not to smoke, and many pay money to join a program or obtain a drug that will help them quit.If many smokers forgive to smoke, then the medical care insurance need for smokers number may be influenced to reduce.

In social benefit view, medical insurance for smokers insurance will be influenced to reduce, due to many smokers forgive to smoke. Although, many smokers may get health, when they do not smoke, they do not pay to buy any cigeratte often, they can save more money, but cigeratte sellers and medical insurance service providers , their income must be influenced to reduce. Hence, when our society government's advertisement concerns smokers often smoke cigeratte, it may bring poor drug health or many cars air pollution, these two messages may influence or dissuade many smokers forgive to smoke or many people do not buy cars. They choose to catch public transportation, or owning car people who do not often drive cares, then car gas or fuel suppliers income will be influenced to reduce, due to many car owning people do not often drive cars or many people do not choose to buy cars. Then, car sellers' income wil be influenced to reduced. Moreover, in long term social influence, when many people do not feel lung disease . Then, the medical care insurance need will also influenced to reduce.

It may bring insurance industry develops in difficulty for lung dissease medical care insurance. So, it explains why consumer behavior may also influence our social economic development in long term . They have cause and effect close relationship. When many consumers individual forgive or dislike to do the behavior in habit, e.g. driving car behavior or smoking behavior. Then, it will influence car seller market and cigeratte seller market to be poor in any countries , even global market.

Hence, in our society, when one individual feels that he.she has individual challenge, it may be economic or emotion or health problem, such as smoking influences health case, driving influences air pollution case. These both kinds of individual behavior may influence the individual may need to spend money for lung disease if he/she has continue smoking habit every day or he/she often drives car . Then, the individual will seek methods to solve these possible occurrence of problems before they do not occur. As it occurs in the natural environment, e.g. air pollution or lung disease is caused by cars or smoking. When individual begins feel these negative effect may case, if he/she continues to do smoking or dirving car behavior. He/she will begins to find methods to solve problem, problem solving is defined as the self-directed cognitive -behavioral process by which an individual , couple or group, such as smokers and drivers group in our society, they attempt to identify or disciver effective solutions for specific problem encountered in everyday living. More specifically, this cognitive -behavioral process (a) makes available a variety of potentially effective solutions for a particular problem and (b) increases the probability of selecting the most effective solution from among the various alternatives (D'Zurilla & Gold field 1971).

reference

D' Zurilla, T. J. & Goldfield, M.R, (1991). Problem solving and behavior
modification, Journal of abnormal psychology, 78, 107-126.

As this definition implies social problem solving is conceived as a conscious, rational, effortful, and purposeful activity. Depending on the problem solcing goals, this process may be aimed at changing the problematic situation for the better, reducing the emotional distress that it produces or both.

Hence, it implies that when any one feels he/she will have individual problem, e.g. health problem , economuc problem,emotion problem. He/she will avoid to continue to do the kind of behavior often every day ,e.g. smoking behavior or driving car behavior .When our society has many people make to forgive to do above themselves behaviors, such as smoking or driving habit. Then, it will influence cigeratte sale number and car sale numner to be reduced. So, when our society has any consumer groups, they forgive to do themselves behaviors in habit. Consequently, the kind of product seller or service provider may lose man customers. So, in our society , when one kind of product or service consumers , their habital behaviors are changed to reduce, then it may influence the kind of product sellers or service providers their income or clients number to be either decrease or increase. On conclusion, it explains that why social behavior has close relationship to influence business income or clients number in our societies.

CHAPTER IV

Tourism industry changing strategy

Our global tourism development had been developed from birth cycle stage to decline life cycle stage nowadays. From 1960 beginning, when airplanes were popular to be increased need to global travelers. Hence, from 1960 to 1970 is whole global tourism industry birth cycle stage. Till to 1971 beginning, many Asia, e.g. Singapore, Japan, China and Western, e.g. UK, UK etc. countries people, they have jobs to do ,and they have more extra money to prepare to choose any leisure activities. From 1971 to 1980, it is growth life cycle stage to global tourism industry. Many airplane manufacturers had been beginning to manufacturer many airplanes because they felt global traveler number would increase. In fact, in this ten years, global traveler number had been increasing every year. Then, from 1981 to 2019 this fourty years, it is global tourism industry nature life cycle stage. It means that every year travel number had been increasing more significantly to compare past. Also, many travelers feel need to travel every year. So, global travel tourism industry may reach the most top travel clients level in this fourty years. However, till to 2020 , due to COVD19 human mouth and disease occurrence, it influences global travelers feel fear to catch air planes to travel because this kind COVD 19 human mouth disease may cause lung disease from air. When many travelers are sitting in the close window air plane, if one person has ths kind COVD19 human mouth disease. The sick person may contact air to let the persons to breath to cause lung disease in possible in airplane. So, global travelers number is decreasing after 2019 . Also, it implies that tourism industry is facing decline life cysle stage.

It brings these questions: IS it right time to develop space tourism? Can space tourism help future tourism industry to re-grow its life cycle stage from nowadays decline life cycle stage? Can space tourism develop to nature stage from birth life cycle stage ? I shall attempt to give evidence to explain whether space tourism may be developed to let human has more one kind tourism . It may be future leisure new trend for travelers, instead of earth travel. Because one day earth tourism destination may not bring leisure interesting to global traveler, then space tourism may be attempted to replace this kind of travelling activity . So, space tourism is birth life cycle stage. However, our earth tourism may define moral tourism, nature tourism, green tourism, responsible tourism in future new travelling leisure trend.

It bring these questions: Can our future tourism industry meet the expectations with the terms " ecological tourist"? Which factors affect the product life cycle of eco tourism? Nature and green tourism may be our earth new kind of travel activities, when many young and old age travelers like to climb mountains, they feel life nature scene more than non-man made) nature scene in their journeys, they do not like to visit cities to travel. It is possible that they often work in offices, this office working factor may influence many travelers like green tourism in the future. So, green or nature tourism will be our future popular tourism leisure activities. It may influence nowadays our tourism decline life stage to re-grown to nature life cycle stage in possible in this COVD19 people mouth disease influential environment.

New economic development in Tourism and oil industries

● How to develop new economic tourism industry

How to develop tourism industry in new economic environment? Any examination of the new economic development of travel and tourism requires definitions of the subject and its components, which are suitable for economic analysis. However, in new economic development to tourism industry, it is also important to look at tourism conceptually, in order to set the scene for a deeper understanding of the future new tourism industry development.

Tourism is neither a phenomenon nor a simple set if industries, however, in new or old economic development environment. It is a human activity which encompasses human behavior, use of resources, and interaction with other people, economies and leisure enjoyment environment. It is also involved physical movement of tourists to locales other than their normal living places.

In future new economic environment, traditional travel needs to include these element in order to satisfy traveler enjoyment and leisure feeling: They may include: Tourist needs and motivations, tourism selection and behavior and constraints , travel away from home , market interactions between tourists and those supplying products to satisfy tourist needs and impacts on tourists , hosts, economies and environments.

In new economic environment, the tourism products may include: carriers, in any forms of transport for tourist travel accommodation, man-made attractions, which could also include the managed areas of natural attractions, private sector and public sector support services, middlemen, such as tour wholesalers and travel agents.

The tourism resources may also include: Natural resources, lands , minerals, water and biological; labor resources, human work, and enterprise; capital resources, manmade enhancement and other resources. The travel and tourism resources problems may include: As there is frequently a mismatch between producer and consumer perception of what constitutes the tourism product , there may be conflict in ideas of which resources are properly involved as well as many of the resources likely to be in demand for tourism are public goods , or even free resources.

In new economic development to tourism industry view, we need to consider that tourism and travel has the reputation of being a relatively clean and pleasant industry in which to work or invest in order to attract a greater number of resource suppliers than as less well-perceived industry, which therefore keeps rewards prices down by competition, how to attract those retiring from or travel business for example, if their finances are already sound, income from travel is not expected to be optimal , travel and tourism is frequently highly seasonal , offering rewards that are competitive with other industries only some of the time, destination products are often in locations which are of little use to other industries, so that competition for resource use if minimal and hence rewards are low.

In general, tourist purpose may include: recreational purpose : holiday, health and sport and religion as well as business purpose: company business , e.g. conventions and sales trips. So, in new economic tourism development aim, tourism industry need consider hoe to achieve incentive trips to let these both tourists to feel. For example, the overall type of tourism required, destination arrangement, travel mode, accommodation and attraction visiting and purchasing method or distribution channel. The purchasing method choices may include: whether to buy an inclusive package or separate service, whether to buy direct from suppliers, such as airlines or hotels or use an agent , which tour wholesaler or operate or agent to use.

I predict the tourism development in new economic view, it may have these characteristics: Few enterprises in travel and tourism are large, highly cashed-up and have a large asset base, enterprises within travel and tourism that are not in a financial position to diversify, and those do well success to the above –average growth obtainable in travel and tourism compared with many other industries, they would therefore tend to expand within the sector. The result of individual enterprise growth and integration within travel and tourism is an increase in the concentration of that industry. The degree to which output is produced of fewer and fewer enterprises. This can be only be accounted for realistically with the context of an individual economy, Levels of concentration in any part of travel and tourism in the future are likely to depend on two opposing factors: The constant demand by many tourist market segments for new experiences and products, which encourages the development and survival of more and diverse enterprises, and therefore leads to the reduction of concentration as well as technology, which in travel and tourism frequently calls for large capital outlays and requires mass markets for efficient use, promotes integrations and large scale enterprise, especially in air travel and non-personal services (marketing and information communication, travel insurance , tourism payment methods). IN these areas, concentration will undoubtedly increase in future new economic development environment.

● How new economic development in oil industry

The future global economic growth, it will influence personal incomes and GDP rise. They would carry different weight in different countries at different times. Starting from low levels of incomer and economic development. Household consumption will change from being dominated by basic heat to rapidly rising energy use for higher levels of comfort in space heating and cooling (and large dwellings), and greater use of electrical appliances, finally to a degree of saturation influenced by the income distribution patterns of the country concerned. Income distribution typically changes very slowly, so that the technical market for heart will never be saturated because there will always be a proportion of poor people living in small spaces less comfortably than the average. Industrial energy consumption will be influenced by technical efficiency within each sector, and by changes in the structures of the economy, e.g. changing proportions of agriculture, heavy and light industry, and services. One may eventually see evidence of diminishing marginal returns to additional energy inputs compared to other inputs. Energy consumption in the energy transformation sector may be influenced by income, which drives the demand for electricity to influenced by income, which drives the demand for electricity to grow faster than the demand for heat, but is also subject to the chosen technology of transformation, which is influenced by the cost and availability of primary energy inputs (fuels) in new economic development environment.

IN new economic development environment, it will influences that fuels do not compete in all sectors; for example, the transport sector is dominated by oil. Nuclear and hydroelectric power (and most renewables) reach the user through electricity; electricity itself competes with the direct burning of fossil fuels. Electricity provides the means by which other fuels can compete with oil and gas in sectors, such as space heating and process heat. It also is the only means of powering applications such as motors, computers and lighting: these subsectors are difficult to analyze. However, there is strong evidence that higher incomes do not weaken the demand for electricity so much as the demand for energy in total (in contrast to the effect on the demand for non-electric energy forms).

Econometricians look at the historical record of change in fuel prices and quantities to distinguish several factors between the new economic development and old economic development to oil industry in the future. An income effect. Increasing (reducing) fuel prices reduces (increases) the purchasing power of consumers' income: higher incomes caused by lower prices will increase energy consumption; the consumers' allocation of the increased income to energy purchases may reduce as income rises. Thus income may be heading in a different direction from fuel prices that the effect of fuel price changes when incomes are rising means simply that rising incomes have increased demand. Reducing the cost of using energy through win-win efficiency measures causes a similar problem . On the consequence, in future new economic development environment, it may influence in both cases demand will be less than if the future oil price or efficiency has not changed. The other effect is that an efficiency or substitution effect. An increase in fuel prices may cause consumers to spend more on new equipment, building materials and management operations, which will reduce the amount of fuel required to give the same energy result to the user. The extent of the efficiency effect depends on what happens to the price of the new equipment or building: if those price s rise in line with the fuel price, changes in the balances between fuel and capital or management will not occur. A new user technology , such as the development of the combined cycle gas turbine generator may increase efficiency and thus greatly reduce the quantity of primary fuel needed to produce the required output in this case electricity. If electricity prices had remained sticky, and the electricity and gas markets were not competitive, some of this advantages could have accrued to the gas suppliers in the form of an increase in price, because th4 unit of gas produces more output of electricity, it would have a higher value. In reality, the development of new economic competitive environment in both gas and electricity has tended to ensure that the benefits of such technical advanced accrue to the consumer through lower final prices. The same many apply in the case of improved efficiency in future non-manual driving auto vehicle development: the consumer's cost of motoring is reduced in new economic non-manual driven auto vehicle (Artificial intelligent vehicle) can replace manual driven vehicle , even electricity battery can replace oil energy to be used in vehicles. So, oil price may be influenced to reduce in future new economic development environment.

New and old economic theories explain oil is not main factor to influence tourism income

● Can economic theory explain old price change to influence tourism income?

I shall attempt to apply old and new economic theory to explain whether oil changing price has direct relationship to influence global tourism indusry development or tourism income as below:

Is oil changing price the main to influence tourism income or tourism development or economic growth ? If oil price rises ar falls, it will or won't cause tourism income decreases or increases? If they have cause and effect relationship, what are the main factors to influence tourism income changes by oil price rises or falls ?

I aim to investigate how any why among oil price shocks will influence tourism income variables. We may distinguish between these oil price shocks: Supply-side , aggregate demand and oil specific demand shocks. I assume that oil specific demand shocks affect inflation and the tourism sector equity index. By constrast, I also believe that aggregate demand oil price shock exercisr an effect, either directly and indirectly tourism generated income and economic growth. So, in old economic theory, supply-side , aggregate demand view to oil specific demand shocks will influence tourism income varies. So, governments ought implement strategies against future oil price movements or plan for economic policy development.

In fact, instead of oil price changes will influence tourism income, it could also harm economic growth and tourism activities, due to the effect they expert on transporation, production cost, economic uncertainty.Because tourism activities is one important sector to influence any country's leisure consumption GDP income source. So, sudden fluctuations in oil prices may also influence economic growth. It is based a hyphthesis known as the tourism led economic growth. So, it seems that they have direct or indirect relationship to case effect between oil price and tourism activities and development. So, increase on tourism income, the called " economic-driven tourism growth". In addition, high oil prices are affecting certain tourism industry segments , e.g. airlines, cruises lines, hotel, rent travelling car services etc. for oil, importing countries example, with reference to macro economic effects, higher oil prices generally lead to higher inflation, when they negatively influence to country's income.

Hence, from a micro-economic perspective, positive oil price shocks lead to a decline in disposable income. for low income people, it will bring an immediate and negative impact on tourism, mainly due to they feel tourism leisure is regarded as a luxury good, when oil price shocks to rise suddenly . It influences any airline or cruise entertainment service providers' costs are influenced to raise. Then, they need to increase air ticket or cruise ticket price. It will bring on negative tourism leisure demands-side the oil price increases low income group, potential tourism leisure consumers. Hence, it seems that oil price may have indirect relationship to influence tourism leisure consumers' needs.

   ● How the price of oil changes influences global tourism industry growth or recession?

In macro-economic view, sudden mid and long term oil price shock can influence global torusim industry growth or recession. For example, a oil price of US$180 per barrel was considered only a few years ago, now this has a realistic scenario to which all plaers in the T&T sector have to adapt. At such a high level, the price of oil will become even more critical to almost every part of the tourism value chain. Although, weak global demand, caused by global economic recesson, resulted in a steep oil price decline to US$45 per barrel by the fourth quarter of 2008 in the past low oil price occurrence history, this won't change the mid to long -term oil forecast.

In fact, the past oil price occurrence history of the dramatic structural had changed a high price imposed on airlines, travelers, and destination countries, all of which will have to navigate through times of shifting or even declining travel demand. I assume that a high oil price scenario is assumed in the long term in order to highlight the changes , such a senario would mean for consumer behavior and the competitiveness of several destinations.

Low oil price in the 1970 and early 1980 did not bring significant growth of international air travel, but its growth has been strongest between 1980 and 2004, a period with stable and relatively moderate oil prices. Also, the rapid development of the low-cost carrier business model in the 1990s further fueled air travel growth by capturing tourism leisure demand , such as weekend leisure travel to cities using mostly secondary airports in any big area countries, such as UK, US . However, the tourism growth is whole influenced by high oil prices, due to oil price had been continue rising in possible.

Basis of oil is shortage supply product, oil is assumed to be the main energy source for the aviation sector for the nest 30 years. Although, second-generation biofuels seem to be on the horizon, the economics as well as the production scalability and aviation biofuel shortage will be a main challenge to airline industry. So, I assume that oil price will continue rise up, if there have none any aviation biofuel can be reflected to oil to use for air plane energy.

Until 2004, the only factors to have affected air travel growth, negatively were in external shocks , such as 9/11, causes catching air plane crisis or US regional geopolitical conflicts. It brings some travelers feel fear to go to US travel, as well as until recently 2019, human mouth disease can influence air to have disease to anyone from mouth. So, global travelers number had been continue decreasing, because they are fear to get disease by air when many themselves every stranger travelers are sitting on the without windows air planes. Although, mouth human and air disease and US 9/11 air attack both matters may influence oil price falls effect, because air planes flying times will reduce. They won't need frequent to fly, to cause aviation oil energy need reduce. Consequently, oil price will decrease, due to travelers number reduces and air planes flying times are also influenced to reduce. (oil demand decreases cause oil price decrease). Although, air lines ' cost will also be influenced reduce, but oil price decrease can not bring travelers number increase , when air ticket price reduce because global many leisure and business trip travelers feel fear to catch air planes frequently when human mouth air disease occured in 2019. So, oil price decreases can not grow up tourism industry growth or rise tourism income.

However, the obvious impact of a high oil price is an increase in the operating costs of airline. Moreover, fuel cost as a percentage of airline operating costs vary significantly based on the length of the flight. The longer the flight, the higher the fuel costs as a percentage of the airline operating cost. So, from an online's perspective, long -hauel flights represent the most criticial challenge to profitable operation because the share of fuel on these flights, compared with other cost items, is largest, because of the unfacorable fuel economics, due to fuel costs even at high-load factors. For example, Thai airways dropped its non-stop Bongkok to US flights in the summer of 2008 for commercial reasons, because fuel reached operating cost levels of 55 percent on this route, a cost burden that could not be passed on to their customers. So, the estimated price elacticity of passengers demand at this Bongkok to US flights route is high, if Thai Airways rises less air ticket price, it will influence many travelers to choose other airlines to catch air plan to fly. Hence, due to Thai Airways can not make decision to rise air ticket price, because it believes that it will lose many travelers, so it only chooses to drop this non-stop Bongkok to US flights to avoid fuel cost rising economic loss.

However, although micro and macro economic theories may also that oil price variable or change, it may influence global tourism income. But, recently, on 2019, human mouth and air diseases, it can influence global individual leisure and business trip travelers feel fear to catch air plans to avoid their bodies get this kind of death sickness when they sit in the no fresh air supplying air planes. They feel that they reduce leisure travelling flying times or business trip flying times with strange travelers to sit in crowd air planes together. Then, they must many avoid human moth and air disease to avoid death crisis. Hence, in this global human mouth and air diseases threat environment occurrence, even oil price sudden reduces to low price, it brings airline's cost reduces and air ticke price reduces. However, when air ticket price reduce to be very cheaper, it can not still attract global many leisure or business trip travelers to buy air tickets to fly frequently. Why does air ticket reduction, it can not attract many leisure or businee trip travelers to buy air ticket to fly ? The main reason is because human mouth and air disease influences global many travelers feel fear to catch air planes frequently. In psychological view, this kind of human mouth and air sickness will bring long time negative influence to global traveles do not want to catch air planes for business trips or travelling leisure frequently. So, it implies that oil price changing to influence air ticket price reduction factor ought not main factor to influence tourism income. It may include traveler individual negative emotion psychological factor, such as human mouth and air disease or 2019 9/11 attack both cases, they can influence global travelers feel fear to catch air planes to fly to avoid death threat. So, oil changing price ought not be only one absolute main factor to influence global tourism income significantly.

On conclusion, in economic view, it seems that oil chang price may have indirect or direct relationship to influence tourism income, instead of some unpredicted external environment factors influence, such as US 9/11 attack crisis and human mouth and air disease factors, they may be main factors to influence travellers number to reduce in non-economic external unpredicted environment view.

How can artificial intelligent tools predict travelling consumer behavior in airline and air agent travelling market

I believe that applying (AI) big data tool to predict vehicle buyer consumption choice behavior, it is similar to predict traveler consumption choice behavior. In this chapter, I shall indicate how to apply (AI) big data gathering tool to predict vehicle buyer consumption choice behavior. Then, I shall its what its similar points to be applied to predict traveler consumption choice behavior.

Nowadays, many vehicle manufacturers hope their vehicles can attract to vehicle buyers to choose to buy their vehicles. However, there are many different brands of vehicles to provide to them to choose, so the vehicle market competition is very serious.

How to judge their different kinds of vehicle price which is reasonable acceptance to attract vehicle buyers to choose to buy the brand of vehicle manufacturers' any kinds of vehicles, e.g. fast speed sport style vehicles, comfortable and slow speed common cars, for four passengers common small size or more than four passengers common large car size?

How to evaluate the vehicle prices issue is important factor to influence vehicle buyers' choices. Either if the brand of vehicle price is too high to compare other brands of similar vehicle price, it will influence many vehicle buyers choose to buy other brands' vehicles or if the brand of vehicle price is too low, it will influence vehicle buyers feel this brand's vehicle machine quality or safe driving level or manufacturing steel material or speed or not comfortable sitting etc. different factors is worse to compare to other vehicle brands' similar vehicle products.

Thus, if the brand of vehicle manufacturers can predict how to design vehicles which can attract many vehicle buyers to choose to buy whose any vehicle products. What are future vehicle buyers' favorable vehicle styles? Then, the vehicle manufacturer can concentrate on manufacturing the kind style of vehicle products to sell already. It will reduce its vehicle manufacturing investment risk.

How to apply (AI) tools to predict vehicle buyers' behavioral consumption model? Whether artificial intelligent tools can predict automotive buyers' behavioral consumption model and predict future vehicle design trend. In fact, automotive brands and dealerships are facing an increasingly competition when attempting to manually gathering the vast quantities of data required to create customer focused programs that increase retention, ultimately new sales and service automotive business.

Building a based on that client's intrinsic needs and interests to any kinds of automotive vehicles at any given time. This is especially true in the automotive industry where the time span between purchases is measured in years. Because vehicle buyers would not like often to change their old vehicle to another new one. So, their decisions to buying another new vehicle, the time is usually after one year, even longer time. Hence, it seems any vehicles won't be frequent consumption products to the owned at least one vehicle family consumers (vehicle buyers). It implies that why vehicle manufacturers ought need to spend time to predict future vehicle buyer design choice for whole year vehicle buyer number growth because they won't often change preferable vehicle design to change another new vehicle more easily.

Hence, how to predict vehicle consumers' taste or preferable which styles of vehicle choices issues is very important. If the vehicle manufacturers can not manufacture any attractive vehicles to sell easily in this year. Then, it will lose time, money in this year because it won't know when the owned least one vehicle users or non-owned any vehicle users who will decide to buy one new vehicle or change another new vehicle ensure. The different brand vehicle dealers will possible wait more than one year to attract them to buy their vehicles if their styles are not attractive to compare other brands of vehicle competitors.

However, artificial intelligence and machine learning can help any vehicle manufacturers to find solution to solve patterns in highly to solve patterns in highly complex data-sets that are beyond the capability of a human brain, and then building and automatically acting on the customer insights it generates.

Given the automotive customer need for individualized communications, this technology is positioned to become a critical component of any successful vehicle retailer's domestic or/and overseas vehicle markets. How can vehicle manufacturers and retailers use (AI) to enhance their vehicle marketing campaigns? How will (AI) affect their vehicle sale marketing strategy? What criteria would they use when selecting on (AI) solution?

Vehicle consumers today are able to quickly access different brands of vehicle information, research vehicle products and reviews, negotiate prices and compare one vehicle brand or retailer to another resulting of the brands of vehicle customers. At the same time, the rise of " big -data mining", wearable devices that track user's every move and preference and greater contextualization in advertising and social media has resulted in consumer expectations of individualized. Thus, it seems that (AI) tools can be used to gather " big-data" and then they can make human's mind to analyze how to design kinds of vehicles to satisfy vehicle buyers' needs.

As automotive vehicle marketers can apply (AI) tools to achieve messaging strategies to meet the needs of this new generation of informed vehicle consumers, using data from a variety of sources to move from a variety of sources to move from mass- messaging to more personalized messages aimed at particular vehicle buyer segments, e.g. fast speed sport vehicle buyer segment, slow speed comfortable small size or large size of buyer segment. However, when 90% of vehicle marketers believe having a single vehicle buyer view is important, only 6% have achieved it.

However, one of the main issues vehicle marketers are facing the lack of capacity to efficiently sift through and analyze the massive vehicle buyer amounts of data required to create vehicle buyer individualized vehicle customer experiences easily. This is especially difficult for automotive dealers, the long periods between purchase cycles, and the highly considered nature of the vehicle purchase means that each vehicle dealer needs to not only track a large number of potential vehicle customers for an extremely long period of time, but each of those vehicle customers will generate a huge amount of different kinds of vehicle behavioral consumption data as they research their next vehicle purchase. However, by choosing the right (AI) technological tools and programs , vehicle dealers can solve this big data gathering challenge into a major advantage.

For Forrester vehicle brand example, vehicle consumers have more power over the Forrester vehicle brand's reputation than ever before. Mayne, L. (2014) indicated that Forrester calls this new (AI) tools is the " age of the vehicle customer", a 20 year business cycle in which the most successful vehicle enterprises will reinvent themselves to systematically understand and serve increasingly powerful vehicle consumers. To win in this new age, Forrester declares companies must become vehicle customer obsessed and the only sustainable competitive advantage is knowledge and engagement with customers, such as (AI) gathering data knowledge.

Thus, the biggest challenge vehicle businesses currently face is not the collection of a large quantity of vehicle consumer data, but what to do with that data once they have it. Even at a large vehicle data research firm, the data sets are often too big for a single analyze, or even a team of analysts to sort through and draw conclusion from. However, enter artificial intelligence and machine learning , an efficient technology solution that can continuously find patterns in highly complex data sets that are way beyond the capacity of a human brain and then automatic drive action based on the customer insights is generated.

What is (AI) machine learning tool? Machine learning is a type of (AI) that learns from data and is not explicitly program. Think Amazon, face book. Machine learning serves up relevant content based on an individual vehicle purchase behavior and experiences. More simply, machine learning is a computer program that can learn relationships between data, subject those learnings to errors functions, and then learn from its errors. The program in effect, trains itself.

Lee, T. (2016) explained that "Thus, (AI) tools can learn deep a more advanced branch of machine learning inspired by how our brain's nervous function, has also been found to be especial effective in identifying patterns from data."

When this way sound is complicated from a vehicle dealer perspective, the implementation of a marketing program driven by artificial intelligence can take care of these tasks in an automatic vehicle fashion with little to no manual intervention required from the staff at time vehicle stores.

In practice at a vehicle dealership, the program will continue track vehicle customer behavior online, merging that data with any offline source (like CRM or DMS data) and then analyze this aggregated vehicle buyer data set to predict what vehicle customer may be shopping for and what information they might like to relevance from different kinds style of vehicle design photos.

Why does travelling market seem to similar to vehicle market which can apply (AI) learning tool to predict travellingconsumer behaviors?

Artificial intelligence refers to complex in vehicle market and travelling entertainment market which is very seem to be applied to predict consumer behaviors.

(AI) machine learning that posses the same characteristics of human intelligence and that have all our sense, all our reason and think just like human vehicle buyer who prefer vehicle purchase choice or travelling consumer who prefer travelling package or travelling destination and airline choice. Besides, machine learning is the practice of using algorithms to collect and examine data, learn from it, and then make a determination or prediction about something in the world.

So, it can be attempted to gather data concerns that travelling consumer past travelling destination choice and air ticket price choice and different travelling package, e.g. high, middle, or low class hotel and foods supply and entertainment places choice in their past travelling journeys.

The machine is " trained" using large amounts of data and algorithms that give it the ability to learn how to automatically perform a task with increasing accuracy. Otherwise, deep learning is primarily based on artificial neural networks inspired by our understanding of the biology of human's brains.

Thus, (AI) big data can gather all these past traveler consumption behavioral choice data to make reference to analyze whether how many travelers will choose to go to the specific travelling destination in any time by the past traveler number record to different travelling destinations, then it can gather the past air ticket sale price to different destinations and past travelling package design to different destinations in order to analyze whether it is the cheap airline ticket price factor or attractive travelling package factor or attractive travelling entertainment etc. in order to predict which factor is the most potential influential factor to they choose to go to the destination to travel in different time within one year. Then, traveler agent or airline can collect these big data to judge how to design their package to attract travelers to go to anywhere to travel or what the main factor influence most of them to choose to visit the destination to travel.

For example, travel agents or airlines can apply "Deep learning" breaks down tasks in ways that enables machines to assist them to predict when travelling consumer choice will be changed and why their travelling choice will change and how their travelling choice will change with increasingly complex tasks.

So, such as why (AI) technology can be applied to predict how travelling consumer behavior changes to bring to judge whether anywhere will be many travelling consumers who will prefer to choose travelling hot destinations next year or next month.

Then, travel agents and airlines can gather overall past travelling consumer data to analyze and conclude the more accurate prediction of different travelling destinations to the number of traveler. Then, they can choose how much air ticket price is more reasonable to charge to the travelling destination or how to design the travelling package which can bring more attractive to the prediction number of different travelling destination travelers in order to achieve to raise the different travelling destination number next year.

Thus, (AI) big data machine learning can help airlines or travel agents to solve how to design any attractive travelling package challenge. A travelling package is both one of the most important and carefully considered travelling entertainment consumption the majority of travelling people will ever make in their lifetime at least one travelling time.

It is also a prediction how travelling package will be designed that tends to be fundamentally tied to a travelling person's travelling destination choice identify and travelling package view of themselves. As the same time, travelling consumers' travelling choice changing lifestyles result in changing travelling destination needs, e.g. the country's young travelers can choose to change non-extreme exciting travelling entertainment package from past extreme exciting travelling entertainment package. Due to personal feeling factor in general. However, I believe that (AI) big data can also be attempted to predict when the country's young travelers will choose to change non-extreme exciting travelling behavior.

It is similar to automotive dealers need to remember that vehicle customers and prospects are individual human beings with risk, complex and ever-changing lives factors, these factors will influence every vehicle consumer why who feels has vehicle purchase need, and how who choose to buy the first vehicle if who decided to buy the first vehicle.

It seems that travelling agents or airlines need to remember that travelling consumers and different features or designs are very traveler beings with risk, complex and ever-travelling package attitude personal changing factors in different travel season, these factor will influence every individual traveler why who feels has travel entertainment need, and how who choose to buy different feature or design travelling package if who decide to travel.

The (AI) big data technological travelling customer behavioral prediction tool seems to be the best travelling behavioral prediction tool in the world are those that know every one of different country's traveler need. Their likes and dislikes which style of travelling package, preferences and travel destination changing tastes to travelling destination choices.

The capacity of the human brain, however, limits us from achieving these different type of travel package sales. In this competitive travelling destination choice entertainment environment, (AI) big data machine learning enables platforms to assist the air ticket and travel package sales team by tracking the travelling consumer behaviors of each travelling customer, learning and memorizing their preferences and predicting their future travelling destination choice and travelling package design needs.

Finally, I recommend that for a travel agent or airline travelling marketing platform to make their travelling customer engagement efficient and fully-functional, I should be able to: applying (AI) tools to track every travelling customer behavior across the web, connecting to a society of data sources, CRM, DMS, third-party, web travelling brands, social traveler email, click etc., aggregating and accurately cross-reference data from a variety of sources, leveraging this data to drive insights on a mass scale, as well as on an individualized basis, driving actions and automatically direct travelling customer engagement via multiple channels based on where each customer is in their travelling individual lifecycle.

Why is (AI) big data gathering tool better than psychological and survey methods to predict traveler individual travel choice behavior?

Prediction travel behavioral consumption from psychology and survey methods.

How to predict travel consumption? It is one question to any travel agents concern to use what methods which can predict how many numbers of travelers where who will choose to go to travel more accurately. I think that who can consider how to predict travel behavioral consumption from psychology and survey travel choice prediction method, but it is better to apply (AI) big data gathering method to predict travel consumer's destination choice more accurate. The reason is as below:

The first reason is that traveller individual travel psychological desire is difficult to predict accurate more than (AI) big data gathering method, it is due that the data is past traveler's destination choice and travel package and ticket price actual data from (AI) big data gathering method. Otherwise, survey investigation is only traveler psychological thinking method. It lacks enough past actual traveler data gathering.

The second reason is that on the weakness of traveler individual psychological thinking view of survey investigation. It has evidence to support the relationship between self-identify threat and resistance to change travel behavior to any travelers, controlling for whose past travelling behavior, resistance to change if a psychological phenomenon of long standing interest in many applied branches of psychology.

Past travelling behavior has been acknowledged as a predictor of future action. Such as travelling behavior that is experienced as successful is likely to be repeated and may lead to habitual patterns. Some psychologists differentiate habit between two concepts, such as goal oriented and automatic oriented both. Although repeated past travelling behavior is addition goal oriented and automatic oriented. Further non-deliberative nature of habit may make appeals to judge and to predict future individual traveler's behavior accurately.

However, repeated one traveler will choose the destination to repeat to travel without a necessary constraint of goal orientation and automatic oriented both. So, it seems that psychological factor can influence any individual traveler why and how who choose to decide to repeat to choose the destination to travel.

So, survey investigation is only the traveler's thinking to answer the travel firm. It is not sure that the traveler's past travel experience is real answer. Otherwise, (AI) big data gathering method is computer gathering method which gather past traveler consumption actual data to analyze and conclude future traveler possible repeated travel destination choice and travel package choice more accurate.

The third reason is that on the strength of (AI) big data gathering method computer statistic view to predict future traveller consumer's destination and travel package choice. It is structural equation modeling is an extremely flexible linear-in-parameters multivariate statistical modeling technique. It has been used in modeling travel behavior and values since about 1980 year. It is a software method to handle a large number of variables, as well as unobserved variables specified as linear combinations (weighted averages) of the observed variable.

Can (AI) big data gather data to predict when climate will change to influence poor travelling behaviours?

(AI) big data tool can predict the flexibility of human travelling behavioral change is at least the result of one such mechanism, our ability to travel mentally in time and entertain potential future. Understanding of the impacts is holidays, particularly those involving travel.

Using focus groups research to explores tourists' awareness of the impacts of travel own climate change, examines the extent to which climate change features in holiday travel decisions and identifies some of the barriers to the adoption of less carbon intensive tourism practices.

The findings suggest many tourists don't consider climate change when planning their holidays. The failure of tourists to engage with the climate change to impact of holidays, combined with significant barriers to behavioral change, presents a considerable challenge in the tourism industry. In the future, computer (AI) big data tool can attempt to predict when the country's climate change to influence travelers to choose to go to the country to travel, e.g. next month or next half year or next year hot travelling destinations.

Tourism is a highly energy intensive industry and has only recently attracted attention as an important contributions to climate change through greenhouse gas emissions. It has been estimated that tourism contributes 5% of global carbon dioxide emissions. There have been a number of potential changes proposed for reducing the impact of air travel on climate change. These include technological changes, market based changes and behavioral changes.

However, the role that climate change plays in the holiday and travel decisions of global tourists. How the global tourists of the impacts travel has on climate change to establish the extent to which climate change, considerations features in holiday travel decision making processes and to investigate the major barriers to global tourists adopting less carbon intensive travel practices.

It will bring this question: Will tourists aware the impacts that their holidays and travel have on climate changes to influence their travelling decision?

When, it comes to understand individual traveler's behavioral change, wide range of conceptual theories have been developed, utilizing various social, psychological, subjective and objective variables in order to model travel consumption behavior. These theories of travel behavioral change operate at a number of different levels, including the individual level, the interpersonal level and community level. Whether pro-environmental behavior can be used to predict travel consumption behavior in a climate change. However, the question of what determines pro-environmental behavior in such a complex one that it can not be visualized through one single framework or diagram.

Despite the potentially high risk scenario for the tourism industry and the global environment, the tourism and climate change ought have close relationship.

However, (AI) big data tool can be applied to find what factors to influence the time of travelers' travelling choices. What are the important factors and variables which can limit tourism? e.g. money, time, family problem, extreme hot or cold weather change, air ticket price, journey attraction etc. variable factors.

Mention of holidays and travel were deliberately avoided in the recruitment process, so as not to create a connection factor to influence traveler's individual mind. However, the dismissal of alternative transportation modes can be conceived as either a structural barrier, in the sense that flying is perhaps the only realistic option to reach long-haul holiday destination, or a perceived behavioral control barriers in that an individual perceives flying as the only option open to whom.

The transportation tool factor will be depend to extent on the distance to the destination. This can also be interpreted in a social perspective as an intention with the resources available where much international tourism is structured around flying. To increase the availability of different transportation modes, tourists could choose holiday destination closer to home.

Finally, also how to predict future travel behavioral consumption. I feel that travel agents need to predict whether any country's random daily variation of weather factor is also important to influence travel behavior. e.g. in weather, temperature, rainfall and snowfall with traffic accidents factors will have relationship to cause travel demand.

Some scientists estimate suggest that when warmed temperatures and reduced snowfall are associated with a moderate decline in non-fatal accidents, they are also associated with a significant increase in fatal accidents. Thus increase in fatalities and temperature. Half of the estimated effect of temperature on fatalities is due to changes in the exposure to pedestrians, bicyclists and motorcyclists as temperature increase.

So, if any countries have rainfall, snowfall and low temperature to cause traffic accidents, whether this accident occurrence will influence the travelers who liking climb snow hills, riding bicycle, running sports who will avoid to travel to these countries' bad weather after occurs. So, why I feel that this natural climate factor will also be one serious factor to influence travel behavioral consumption. However, (AI) big data tool can predict more accurate than survey method when climate change to influence the country's climate to be poor, then it can predict when which countries are not popular acceptable to global country consumers' travel choice next month.

How can apply (AI) to provide travelling businesses with better-informed decisions ?

I shall explain how (AI) big data gathering technology can provide travelling businesses with better-informed decisions to drive top-line growth, deliver meaningful experience for travelling customers and smooth their path along the travelling consumer journey. The widely understood definition of (AI) involves the ability of machines or computers to learn human thinking, reasoning and decision-making abilities.

So, such as (AI) learning machine system can attempt to learn travelling consumer's travel destination or travel package thinking, judgement of their reasons why they choose to go to the destination to travel or why they choose to buy the travel package and learn how and why they make their past travelling decisions from their past travel big data gathering.

A Narrative science study in 2015 year identified that (AI) was being used primarily in voice recognition, machine learning virtual assistants and decision support. This study also highlighted the many branches of (AI) and that techniques and their definition are used interchangeably. It is possible that (AI) can be used to gather big data , then to analyze to help travel businesses to predict travelling consumer travel destination and travel package choice behaviors. For example, one of the most common techniques is traveler machine learning, where algorithms are used to perform tasks by learning from the airline or travel agent whose past all travelers' travelling destination choice and travel package choice historical data.

However, during 2017 year, search engines will begin to find what additional factors can influence past traveler personal travelling destination and travelling package travelling behavioral data into prediction of future travelling customer behavioral results, such as the online traveler (user's) history of travelling data searches, such as anywhere are the most popular travelling locations or travelling destinations and previously captures conservations.

Artificial intelligence will use this past travelling destinations and travelling package information to power predictive search results, e.g. predictive future travelling consumer's choice behavioral processing for where will be their preferable travelling destination choice and how to design travelling package to satisfy future travelling clients' needs. Predictive search will improve the quality of online travelling search results, and provide new insights into travelling consumers' travelling destination and package behavior and the moments which matter to them. Search will give recommendation into tailored how travelling consumer individual travelling destination choice in travelling decision making process. Several of the largest online platforms already use (AI) travelling machine learning to improve predictive travelling consumer behavioral search results.

For example, Google's rank brain technology adds research by understanding the context in which the travelling consumer has entered it. Over time, rank brain will learn further from user behaviors Amazon's DSSTNE (pronouned destiny) learns from shoppers' purchasing habits and consumption behavior to offer better product recommend actions, which Amazon can offer before a consumer has entered anything into the search bar.

Such as (AI) big data can gather past online travelers' e-ticket purchase transactions to conclude that online traveler's travelling choice habits and online traveler consumption behavior to offer better travelling destinations and travelling package opinions to travel agents or airlines. However, this technology is not independent of human input. For example, Google engineers will periodically retain the rank brain system to improve the models it uses.

For another example, in 2016 year , Apple computer revamped its travelling scene photos app to allow travelling consumers to search for specific travelling destinations in the travelling scene phots, they want to find anywhere travelling destination photos, not just dates and locations. Each travelling photo that an intelligent phone or intelligent pad user takes goes through 11 billion computations, so that travelling scene photos can understand exactly where is the travelling destination photography to let online travelling consumer to feel anywhere they plan to go to the location to travel. So, (AI) learning machine can make online travelling photos more attractive to influence potential travelers choose to the destination to travel after they see the travelling destination scene photos from internet.

It seems that in future, (AI) machine learning will allow online travelling search to evolve even further. Search engineers will deliver refined recommendations to airlines' online traveler e-ticket search users and use less human input to predict travelling consumers' needs from internet channel. For IBM computer example, it indicated 90% of the data that exists today has been created in the last two years.

This huge explosion of past traveler's e-ticket consumption data gives the opportunity to quickly spot and react to the latest trends, fashion and fads among its travelling clients and potential clients. This will allow airline or travel agent companies to better engage with younger travelling consumers, who gain influence access to the latest travelling destination and package trends.

They associate with to help define who they are as individuals. Thus, travelling company brands have to identify and make use of them before travelling consumers move on, but the vast quantity of past e-ticket purchase data available makes from internet channel. This a resource-intensive task. For next example, Lesara, a based online clothes store, uses this machine learning to inform its product decision often gathering information from internal and external sources.

When its trends -spotting shoes. Lesara has a range of over 20 styles and sells hundreds of pairs a day. It focus on giving consumers, the very latest trends allow Lesara to develop on average of 50,000 new items each year. It compared to 11,000 old items each year. Thus, travelling agents or airlines can attempt to apply (AI) big data gathering method to gather all past e-ticket purchase data, concerns where they prefer to choose to go to the destinations to travel and what travelling packages are the most attractive to the travelers to choose to buy. It aims to help them to predict where future travelers will prefer to choose to go to travel or what travelling package they will prefer to choose to buy next year.

For another (AI) big data prediction example, Lesara is one online clothes store, uses machine learning decisions after gathering information from internal and external sources. One of its most popular products, shoes with LED started life when its trend spotting software flagged up a blogger wearing similar shoes. Now Lesara has a range of over 20 styles and sells hundreds of pairs a day. Its focus on giving consumers the very latest trends allows Lesara to develop an average of 50,000 new items each year, compared to 11,000 for its competitor Lara.

It seems (AI) big data gathering machine learning can help Lesara business to predict what kinds of shoes design or style that shoe consumers will prefer choose to buy in future shoe market trend. Thus, Lesara can predict shoe consumers' taste successfully and it can manufacture many attractive style of shoes.

(AI) machine learning can gather global past shoe consumer's shoe shopping experiences, then analyzes to make conclusion to give lesara recommendation successfully. This will make the experience more enjoyable for shoe consumers and allow Lesara to advert whose different new style or design of shoes to deliver them move relevant messages by understanding the context of the experience.

So, online travel agents or online airline can also attempt to apply (AI) big data gathering method to predict where travelers will prefer to go to travel and how they ought design travelling packages to attract them to choose to buy next year. Hence, (AI) big data gathering technology can conclude how to design traveler agents' travelling package products to be the most attractive to excite many travelers choose to buy their travelling package, due to it has more accurate to predict travelling consumer destination and travelling package choice behaviors to compare human themselves prediction judgement effort, e.g. travelling survey or marketing research, or telephone enquire. It seems that (AI) machine judgement effort is more accurate to compare to human judgment effort in travelling industry.

Future travel consumption behavior

Can (AI) big data gathering tool predict traveler individual habitual behavior , e.g. renting travel transportation tools ?

Can (AI) big data gathering tool can predict past traveler destination and travelling package choice habit and it can be intended to predict of future traveler behavior to people are creatures of habits judgement of future anywhere travelling destination choice next year or next month or next half year destination prediction ?

Many of human's everyday goal-directed behaviors are performed in a habitual fashion, the transportation made and route one takes to work, one's choice of breakfast. Habits are formed when using the some behavior frequently and a similar consistency in a similar context for the some purpose whether the individual past travel consumption model will be caused a habit to whom. e.g. choosing whom travel agent to buy air ticket or traveling package; choosing the same or similar countries' destinations to go to travel ; choosing the business class or normal (general) class of quality airlines to catch planes.

Does habitual rent traveling car tools use not lead to more resistance to change of travel mode? It has been argued that past behavior is the best predictor of future behavior to travel consumption. If individual traveler's past consumption behavior was always reasoned, then frequency of prior travel consumption behavior should only have an indirect link to the individual traveler's behavior. It seems that renting travel car tools to use is a habit example. So, a strong rent traveling car tools useful habit makes traveling mode choice. People with a strong renting of traveling car tools of habit should have low motivation to attend to gather any information about public transportation in their choice of travelling country for individual or family or friends members during their traveling journeys.

Even when persuasive communication changes the traveler whose attitudes and intention, in the case of individual traveler or family travelers with a strong renting travel car tools habit. It is difficult to change whose travel behaviors to choose to catch public transportation in whose any trips in any countries. However, understanding of travel behavior and the reasons for choosing one mode of transportation over another. The arguments for rent traveling car tools to use, including convenience, speed, comfort and individual freedom and well known.

Increasingly, psychological factors include such as, perceptions, identity, social norms and habit are being used to understand travel mode choice. Whether how many travel consumers will choose to rent traveling car tools during their trips in any countries. It is difficult to estimate the numbers. As the average level of renting travel car tools of dependence or attitudes to certain travel package policies from travel agents. Instead different people must be treated in different ways because who are motivated in different ways and who are motivated by different travel package policies ways from travel agents.

In conclusion, the factors influence whose traveler's individual traveler destination choice behavior The factors include either who chooses to rent traveling car tools or who chooses to catch public transportation when who individual goes to travel in alone trip or family trip. It include influence mode choice factors, such as social psychology factor and marketing on segmentation factor both to influence whose transportation choice of behavior in whose trip. So, (AI) big data can be attempted to gather past traveler transportation tool choice, rent travelling car tools choice or catching public transportation tools choice to predict where destination can provide what kind of transportation tool to attract many travelers to choose to go to the place to travel.

How (AI) big data determine future travel behavior from past travel experience and perceptions of risk and safety for the benefits to travel consumers?

How (AI) big data determine future travel behavior from past travel experience and perceptions of risk and safety for the benefits to travel consumers? Why does individual traveler avoid certain destination(s) is(are) as relevant to tourist decision making as why who chooses to travel to others?

Perceptions of risk and safety and travel experience are likely to influence travel decisions. If travel agents had efforts to predict future travel behavior to guess whether travelers will feel where is(are) risk and unsafe to cause who does not choose to go to the country to travel. Then, the travel agents will avoid to choose to spend much time to design the different traveling package to attract their potential travel consumers to choose to travel. The reason is because in the case of individual traveler's tourism experience, the traveler whose past disappointment travel experience (

psychological risk) will be a serious threat to the traveler's health or life (health, physical or terrorism risk). The past safety or unhealthy risk to the country(countries) will influence the traveler decides to choose not to go to the countries(country) to travel again in the future.

What is push and pull factors to influence any traveler who chooses where is whose preferable travelling destination ?

How to apply (AI) big data to predict individual traveler's behavioral intention of choosing a travel destination? Understanding why people travel and what factors influence their behavioral intention of choosing a travel destination is beneficial to tourism planning and marketing. In general, an individual's choice of a travel destination into two forces.

The first force is the push factor that pushes an individual away from home and attempt to develop a general desire to go somewhere, without specifying where that may be.

The other force is the pull factor that pull an individual toward in destination, due to a region-specific or perceived attractiveness of a destination. The respective push and pull factors illustrate that people travel because who are pushed by whose internal motives and pulled by external forced of a destination. However, the decision making process leading to the choice of a travel destination is a very complex process.

For example, a Taiwanese traveler who might either choose new travel destination of Hong Kong or another old travel Asia destinations again or who also might choose any one of Western country, as a new travel destination. The travel agents can predict where who will have intention to choose to travel from whose past behavior and attitude, subjective and perceived behavioral control model. When (AI) big data gather past every country traveler number who chose to go to which countries to travel in order to judge where destinations will be the country travelers' travelling choice destinations in the future.

The factors influence where is the traveler choice, include personal safety, scenic beauty, cultural interest, climate changing, transportation tools, friendliness of local people, price of trip, trip package service in hotels and restaurants, quality and variety of food and shopping facilities and services etc. needs. So, whose factors will influence where is the individual travel's choice. It seems every traveler whose choice of travel process, will include past behavior. e.g. travelling experience, travelling habit, then to choose the best seasoned travelling action to satisfy whose travel needs. This process is the individual traveler's psychological choice process, who must need time to gather information to compare concerning of different travel packages, destination scene, climate change, transportation tools available to the destination, air ticket price etc. these factors, then to judge where is the best right destination to travel in the right time.

Hence, (AI) big data can gather past different countries' climate changing data, transportation tool changing data, destination scene environment changing etc. different data to give opinions to travelling businesses whether any country's these above factors will influence about how many traveler number will be increase or decrease in the future.

Why can expectation, motivation and attitude factor influence travelling behavior?

Social psychology is concerned with gaining insight into the psychological of socially relevant behaviors and the processes. For instance, on a global level bad influence to global warming, it influences some countries extreme cold or hot bad climate changing occurrence, then it ought influence some travelers' behavioral decision to change their mind to choose some countries to go to travel at the moment which do not occur extreme hot or cold climate (temperature). e.g. above than 40 degree in summer or below than 0 degree in winter. Due to the extreme climate changing environment in the countries, it will cause them to feel uncomfortable to play during their trips. So, the global warming causes to climate changing factor will influence the numbers of travel consumption to be reduced possibly. This is global climate changing environment factor influences to bad or uncomfortable social psychological feeling to global travelers' mind of traveling decision. What is individual traveler expectation, motivation and attitude? Tourism sector includes inbound (domestic) tourism and outbound (overseas) tourism both incomes to any countries. According to recent article, a tourist behavior model has been developed, called the expectation, motivation and attitude (EMA) model (Hsu et al., 2010).

This model focuses on the pre-visit stage of tourists by modeling the behavioral process by incorporating expectation, motivation and attitude. Travel motivation is considered as an essential component of the behavioral process, which has been increasing attention from the travel; industry. The economic approach defines "tourism" is an identifiable nationally important industry. It includes the component activities of transportation, accommodation, recreation, food and related service. So, tourism behavioral consumption is concerned the individual tourist's usual habituate of the industry which responds to whose needs, and of the impacts that both the tourist and the tourism industry have on the socio-cultural, economic and physical environment.

However, travel motivation means how to understand and predict factors that influence travel decision making. According to Backman and others (1995, p.15), motivation is conceptually viewed as " a state of need, a condition that services as a driving force to display different kind of behavior toward certain types of activities, developing preferences, arriving at some expected satisfactory outcome." So, motivation and expectancy which has close relationship to any tourist before who decided to do any tourism of behavior.

Some economists confirmed motivation and expectancy which has relations, such as expectation of visiting an outbound destination has a direct effect on motivation to visit the destination; motivation has a direct effect on attitude toward visiting the destination; expectation of visiting the outbound destination has a direct affection on attitude toward visiting the destination and motivation has a mediating effect on the relationship in between expectation and attitude.

Hence, (AI) big data can gather all the country's climate environment change, transportation tool change, entertainment scene change, hotel price and restaurant price change etc. data to give opinions whether the country will attract how many traveler to choose to go to travel in the year.

What is (AI) deep learning techniques to forecast travelling environment behavioral consumption

Prediction how many travelers will choose to go to the country to travel. It is similar to apply deep-learning technology to predict how to raise the agricultural farming productivity in the agricultural export country.

The (AI) deep-learning technology leads to performance enhancement and generalization of artificial intelligent technology. It influences the global leader in the field of information technology has declared its intention to utilize the deep-learning technology to solve environmental problems, such as climate change.

So, it will help agriculture farming businesses can raise any plant food: vegetable, fruit, rice which grow up very easily if farmers can apply (AI) deep-learning technology to solve environment problems to influence their plant food grow. If the whole year seasonal change is very good and it is suitable for any plant food to grow in farming land easily, e.g. rain is enough and soil is enough for any plant food to grow in the farm lands. Then, fruit, rice, vegetable etc. agriculture businesses will have much beneficial attribution to global farmers.

The question is how to use deep-learning technologies in the environmental field to predict the status of pro-environmental consumption. We predicted the pro-environmental consumption index based on Google search query data, using a recurrent neural network (RNN model). To certify the accuracy of the index, we compared the prediction accuracy of the RNN model with that of the ordinary least square and artificial necessary network models.

For example, the RNN model predicts the pro-environmental consumption index better than any other model. we expect the RNN model to perform still better in a big data environment because the deep-learning technologies would be increasingly as the volume of data grows. So, deep-learning technologies could be useful in environmental forecasting to prevent damage caused by climate change to influence any rice, vegetable, tomato, potato, fruit etc. different plant food grow in any countries' farming land easily.

For South Korea example, over 800 government agencies spent 2.2 trillion Korea won on eco-products in 2014 year. However, green products are rarely purchased outside these agencies. This phenomenon occurs because there is a gap between consumer attitudes and behavior , that is environmental attitude is a major factor in decision making vis-a-vis the consumption of " green" food and services (Jorea Ministry of Environment, 2015).

Therefore, it is necessary to understand those consumer attitude, that will lead to sustainability-conductive behavior and consumption. (AI) Deep learning system can be applied to attempt understand those traveler attitude to environment protection to fly to which country. For example, (AI) deep learning system can attempt to gather data concerns how many Hong Kong people concern air pollution challenge to influence their health, then it can attempt to predict how many Hong Kong travelers do not choose to go China travel, due to the air pollution challenge to influence their health.

Environmental travel consumption prediction

Recently, many researchers have studied pro-environmental consumption and household indexes as well as suicide rate predictions using messages posted by internet users on Google trend, Tweets etc. channel.

Whether can environmental consumption be predicted by (AI) deep-learning technological internet channel to influence how many travelers choose to go to the country to travel?

How can impact the pro-environmental consumption attitudes of green policies to influence how many travelers choose to go to the country to travel?

For example, Korea scientists estimated pro-environmental attitudes using search query data provided by Google trend and confirmed through regression analysis, that pro-environmental attitude has a positive correlation with the pro-environmental attitude index. They also explained that environment-friendly attitude of residents plan an important role in policy making. In the past, most household consumption indexed were calculated through surveys, but (AI) deep-learning technological tool " big data" have recently gained research attention (Lee et al. 2016). So, (AI) deep learning technology can attempt to gather whether how many Korea residents who concern environment pollution to influence their eating green food attitude then to judge whether how many Korea residents hope to leave their country to travel anywhere either high risk environment pollution countries to travel or low risk environment pollution countries to travel in the future.

It seems that (AI) deep-learning technology can help agricultural export countries' farmers , e.g. US, UK, Canada, New Zealand, Australia, Japan, China, India etc. they can predict environmental behavioral consumption to any rice, tomato, potato , fruit, vegetable etc. plant food consumers. The beneficial advantages to them include as below:

(a) Assuming they know their countries' weather, when it has less rain to cause drought or when it has more rain in any seasonal time in the year. They can choose not to grow any kinds of above these plant food to avoid loss.

(b) They can make any kinds of above these plant food price raising after their prediction of these bad seasonal time to cause their plant food shortage supply challenge. Because these plant food consumers' demand number is more, but the supply of these above plant food supply number is less. However, due to they had predicted when the bad seasonal time can not allow them to grow these above plant food before. So, they have enough time to grow many these above plant food number in predictive good seasonal time to prepare to supply to their plant food import countries' plant food consumers to eat. Thus, these predictive environmental consumption plant food export countries can raise their plant food price to sell to them. When, the other non-pre-predictive environmental consumption plant food export countries can not supply any one of those plant food to them to eat, due to the bad climate to cause them can't grow any one of these plant food to export to sell.

Thus, (AI) deep-learning technology can be applied to predict how to raise the plant food supply number in order to raise price to the import plant food countries consumers to eat, due to they feel difficult to buy these plant food to eat in the bad climate seasonal time in whole year.

(c) (AI) deep-learning technology can help climate scientists to find what reasons cause their countries; rain sudden increases or cause their countries' rain sudden decreases. After its gathering data analysis, it can assist climate scientists to find solution methods to attempt to control the rain level can be right falling down level to let agricultural export farmers who can grow their plant food to sell to agricultural import countries in whole year.

(d) The agricultural export countries' farmers can apply (AI) deep-learning technology to help them to choose whether growing which kinds of plant food in that whether climate time to earn more plant food consumption number more easily.

Due to the agricultural countries climate will often change, for example, tomato, potato, rice, fruit etc. plant food can be adapt to grow in more rain time, but vegetable can not be adapt to grow in more rain time. If farmers can apply this technology to predict when it will have move rain or when it will have less rain to fall down in their countries.

Then, they can choose to grow which kinds of plant food number more, in the suitable seasonal climate time in order to raise plant food growing number productivities to supply to sell to satisfy any agricultural food import countries' demand effectively.

(e) (AI) deep-learning technology can help agricultural import countries to solve agricultural food shortage challenge in long term. When this technology can be popular to base applied by the agricultural plant food export countries. It will solve global agricultural food shortage challenge. For example, when one agricultural export countries' farmers can popular accept to apply this technology to predict when to grow which kinds of plant food more to rise number productivities to sell. e.g. vegetable, fruit, rice Besides another agricultural export countries' farmers can also accept to apply this technology to predict when to grow plant food, e.g. potato, tomato to raise number productivities to sell. Then, they can concentrate on growing the specific kinds of plant food in order to raise the specific plant food number productivities in every seasonal change time every month. Then, global agricultural plant food supply must be raised, due to these predictive environmental change farmers can know who ought grow which kinds of plant food to sell to raise number productivities.

Consequently, (AI) deep learning can gather where countries will have high risk environment pollution to influence health food supply. Then, it can give opinions to travelling businesses when these high risk environment pollution countries will encounter the traveler number to be decreased, due to the environment pollution serious challenge will occur.

What methods can predict future travel behavioral consumption ?

How to use qualitative of travel behavioral method to predict future travel consumption from (AI) big data ?

I also suggest to use qualitative of travel behavioral method to predict future travel consumption. Methods such as focus groups interviews and participant observer techniques can be used with quantitative approaches on their own to fill the gaps left by quantitative techniques. These insights have contributed to the development of increasingly sophisticated models to forecast travel behavior and predict changes in behavior in response to change in the transportation system. I shall indicate the weaknesses of human travelling investigation methods as below:

First, survey methods restrict not only the question frame but the answer frame as well, anticipating the important issues and questions and the responses. However, these surveys methods are not well suited to exploratory areas of research where issues remain unidentified and the researched seek to answer the question "why?".

Second, data collection methods using traditional travel diaries or telephone recruitment can under represent certain segments of the population, particularly the older persons with little education, minorities and the poor. Before the survey, focus group for example can be used to identify what socio-demographic variables to include in the survey, how best to structure the diary, even what incentives will be most effective in increasing the response rate.

After the survey, focus, focus groups can be used to build explanations for the survey results to identify the "why" of the results as well as the implications. One Asia Pacific survey research result was made by tourism market investigation before. It indicated the travel in Asia Pacific market in the past, had often been undertaken in large groups through leisure package sold in bulk, or in large organized business groups, future travelers will be in smaller groups or alone, and for a much wider range of reasons.

Significant new traveler segments, such as female business traveler. The small business traveler and the senior traveler, all of which have different aspirations and requirements from the travel experience.

Moreover, Asia tourism market will start to exist behaviors in the adoption of newer technologies, a giving the traveler new ways to manage the travel experience, creating new behaviors. This with provide new opportunities for travel providers. The use of mobile devices, smartphones, tablets etc. and social media are the obvious findings to become an integral part of the travel experience. Thus, quality method can attempt to predict Asia Pacific tourism market development in the future. It is such as (AI) big data gathering tool can give traveler quality opinions to any travelling businesses to make the more accurate where will be the popular travel destination choice next month or next half year or next year.

However, improving the predictive power of travel behavior models and to increase understanding travel behavior which lies in the use of panel data(repeated measures from the same individuals). Whereas, cross-sectional data only reveal inter-individual differences at one moment in time, panel data can reveal intra-individual changes over time. In effect, panel data are generally better suited to understand and predict (changes in) travel behavior. However, a substantial proportion was also observed to transition between very different activity/travel patterns over time, indicating that from one year to the next, many people renegotiated their activity/travel patterns.

How to apply advanced traveler information systems (ATIS) to predict future travelling behavior?

Nowadays, information can impact on traveler behavior and network performance. For example, when steadily growing levels of vehicle ownership and vehicle miles traveled information has been identified as a potential strategy towards man aging travel demand, optimizing transportation networks and better utilizing available capacity. Toward, this goal to predict further tourist behavioral consumption. Many countries, government tourism development institutes has applied advanced traveler information systems (ATIS) which travel behavior models and high-fidelity network performance models made increasingly feasible through the rapid advances in computer power. Crucial components of this problem domain are the modeling of individual tourist drivers' response to travel information and the development accurate guidance of relevance to real would trip makers. So, this advanced traveler information systems (ATIS) can assist the tourist who like to rent travelling car tools to travel in any countries own free traveler information systems service conveniently. Also, this travel information system can be intended to assist travelers to make better travel choices. e.g. this system can improve the decision making of individual traveler rather than improvements of network performance overall. So, we need to understand how tourists make their travel plans. Also, understanding decision process that lead to booking of the trip is equally important, as it allows of a potential behavior.

How can online tourism sale channel influence traveling consumption of behavior?

Nowadays, internet is popular, it seems that booking air ticket behavior of using internet is predicted to influence overall tourism air tickets payment method. Tourism industry has grown in the previous several decades. Despite its global impact, questions related to better understanding of tourists and whose habits. Using online travel air ticket booking benefits include booking electronic air tickets can be made from entering any electronic travel agents websites in the short time and electronic travel ticket payers do not need leave home, who can pay visa card to pre booking any electronic travel ticket from online channel conveniently.

How can analyze activity based travel demand ?

Nowadays, human are concerning the traffic congestion and air quality deterioration, the supply oriented focus of transportation planning has expanded to include how to manage travel demand within the available transportation supply. Consequently, there has been an increasing interest in travel demand management strategies, such as congestion pricing that attempts to change aggregate travel demand. The prediction aggregate level, long term travel demand to understanding disaggregate level (i.e. individual levels) behavioral responses to short term demand policies, such as ride sharing incentives, congestion pricing and employer based demand management schemes, alternate work schedules, telecommuting limitation of travel agent traditionally work nature shall influence oriented trip based travel modelling passenger travel demand indirectly.

Finally, online travel purchase will be popular to influence the number of travel behavioral consumption nowadays. Any travel package products can be sold from websites to attract travelers to choose to pre-book air ticket for any trips conveniently. In the past ten years, the internet has become the predominant carrier of all types of information and transactions. Regarding travel decisions, internet has also become an important sales channels for the travel industry, because it is associated with comparably lower distribution and sales costs, but also because it adapts to high supply and demand dynamics in this industry. Consequently, the travel and tourism industry tries to increase the internet sale specific share of sales volumes. So, internet sale channel has changed travel consumption behavioral pattern and characteristics and travel experience. For example, Switzerland has one of the highest population-to-computer ratio in Europe. It is also one of the most highly internet penetrated countries in terms of use of the WWW on a day-to-day basis, with more than 75 percent of the population older than 14 years using the WWW daily (ICT, 2005).

The reason of booking online tourism may include: convenience, fast transaction, finding traveling package choice easily, more airline seats available. So, online booking tourism will influence the traditional tourism agents visiting of sales and air tickets and travelling package numbers to be decreased. Finally, the online booking tourism market shares will be expanded to more than traditional tourism agents visits sale market in the future one day. So, the travel agents who still use the traditional tourism visiting sale channel which ought raise whose features to compare to differ to online tourism sale channel if these traditional tourism agents want to keep competitive ability in tourism industry for long term.

What is actively based patterns of urban population of travel behavioral prediction method?

Actively based patterns of urban population. It is a method of motivational framework means in which societal constraints and inherent individual motivations interact to shape activity participation patterns. It can be used to predict one city or urban the numbers of travel demand in the year. It has two elements: First, capability constraints refer to constraints are imposed by biological needs, such as eating and sleeping and/or resources, such as income, availability of cars etc. to undertake the urban or city's family activities in the year. Second, coupling constraints define where, when and the duration of planning activities that are to be pursued with other individuals. So, this method needs to gather information (data) to get the relationship between activities, travel and spending work time and space time to evaluate whether there are how many families who have real needs to spend time to go to travel in the year.

What is trip based versus activity based approaches?

What is trip based versus activity based approaches? The fundamental difference between the trip-based and activity based approaches is that the former approach directly focuses on trips without explicit recognition of the motivation or reason for the trips and travel. The activity based approach , on the other hand, views travel as a demand derived from the need to pursue travel activities. So, it is better understand the individual or family behavior basis for individual or family travelling decision regarding participation in travelling activities in certain places or cities or countries at given times and hence the resulting travel needs. This behavioral basis includes all the factors that influence the why, how, when and where of performed activities and resulting individuals and household, the cultural/social norms of the community and the travel surrounding environment.

Another difference between the two approaches is in the way travel is represented. The trip based approach represents travel as a collection of trips. Each trip is considered as independent of other trips, without considering the inter-relationship in the choice attributes , such as time, destination and mode of different trips. As tours are chains of trips beginning and ending at a same location , say home or work. The tour based representation helps maintain the consistency across and capture the interdependency and consistency of the modeled choice attributed among the trips of the same tour.

In addition to the tour based representation of travel, the activity based approach focuses on sequences or patterns of activity participation and travel behavior, using the whole day or longer periods of time is the unit of analysis. Such as approach can address travel demand management issues through an examination of how people modify their activity participation, for example, will individuals substitute more out-of-home activities for in home activities in the evening of who arrived early form work due-to a work schedule change?

The major difference between trip based and the activity based approaches is in the way, the time dimension of activities and travel is considered. In the trip based approach, time is reduced to being simply a cost making a trip and a day's viewed as a combination, defined peak and off peak time periods. On the other hand, activity based approach views individuals' activity travel patterns are a result of their time use decisions with a continuous time domain. As individuals have 24 hours in a day or multiples of 24 hours for longer periods of time and decide how to use that travel among or allocate that time to activities and travel and with who, subject to their socio-demographic, transportation system and other and scheduling of trips. So, determining the impact of travel demand management policies on time use behavior is an important step to assessing the impact of such policies on individual travel behavior. The final major difference between this two approaches relates to the level of aggregation. In the trip based approach, most aspect of travel, e.g. number of trips etc. are analyzed at an aggregate level.

Consequently, trip based methods accommodate the effect of socio-demographic attributes of households and individuals in a very limited fashion, which limits the activity of the method to evaluate travel impacts of long term socio-demographic characteristics of the individuals who actually make the activity travel choices and the travel service characteristics of the surrounding environment. So, the activity based models are better equipped to forecast the longer term changes in travel demand in response composition and the travel environment of urban areas. Also, using activity based models, the impact of policies can be assessed by predicting individual level behavioral responses instead of employing trip based statistical averages that are aggregated over defined demographic segments.

Can apply (AI) big data gathering method predict senior age will be main travelling target?

In the past, Germany government had established tourism survey analysis to analyze survey data in order to arrive at reliable conclusions on future trends in travel behavior. To aim to find how demographic change will influence the tourism market and how the industry can adapt to those changes. The travel analysis provided data on tourism consumer behavior, including attitudes, motives and intentions. Since, 1970 year, it is based on a random sample, representative for the population in private households aged 14 years or older. Then, a continuous high scientific standard combined with a national and international users makes the travel analysis a useful tool and reliable source for tourism industry and policy decisions. It aimed to gather statistical data. e.g. on the age structure and on demographic trends, quantitative and qualitative analysis with time series data from the travel analysis. It shows e.g. not only the future volume , quite different from today's seniors, or how who will travel of family holidays will change, e.g. single parents of low, but grandparents of growing significance for tourism.

Demographic change is said to be one of the important drivers for new trends in consumer traveling change behavior in most European countries (e.g. Lind 2001). Because the growing number of senior citizens in the European Union and other industrialized countries, such as the USA and Japan, looks to become one of the major marketing challenges for the tourism industry. United Nations statistics predict that the share of people being 60 age or older will grow dramatically in the coming future, and is expected to rise from 10 percent of the world population in 2000 year to more than 20 percent in 2050 year (United Nations Population Division, 2001). From its statistic, some data showed that travel propensity increased throughout life until the age of about 50 years of age and was then kept stable until very late in life 75 age. The most important results is that the travel propensity when getting older is not going down between 65 and 75 age of course, the overall development of this variable is influenced by a lot of other factors which are responsible for quite a variation over time. It is now possible to suggest that the general pattern of travel propensity is one of the key indicators for holiday life cycle travel behavior, includes three stages. The growth stage tends to increase from early adult hood until 45 age old or when reaching some 80%. The next stage is stabilization from the ages of around 50 age, until 75 age old, starting with a lower increase. Finally, the decrease stage is a slight decrease occurs once people reach the more advanced age of 75 age to 85 age old (Lohmann & Danielsson 2001).

So, it seems Germany government tourism prediction to future travelers' behavior indicated these findings, such as on how future senior generations will travel, who had used survey data to examine the patterns of travel behavior of a generation getting older and applied the findings to draw conclusions on the future. Also, it predicted that on the future of family trips, family segmentation will be the travel behavior patterns in the future. These findings together with the statistical data on demographic change allowed for a better understanding of the coming tends in family holidays. It's aim developed in consumer behavior related to demographic change and predicted what will happen future of tourism one had to consider other influences and drivers as well, for example, trends on the supply side. e.g. low cost airlines or in travelling consumption behavior in general whether how the past may provide a key to predict travel patterns of senior citizens to the future.

Given the projected growth of the senior citizens market, designing specific marketing strategies to meet the prospective needs of elderly tourists will become increasingly important. It has been an implicit assumption that it will be a close relationship between the travel behavior of today's senior citizens and the those of future ones. The growing number of senior citizens in the world. e.g. China, Hong Kong, Japan, USA etc. countries. Global senior citizen tourism market will be based solely on demographic predictions about the future of the population's age structure. However, many of these seniors won't only live longer but will be fitter and more active until later in life. Many of the will also have plenty in life. Many of them will also have plenty of time and money to spend on travel. So, will these new seniors behave like today's senior citizens? Will they adopt the same travel behavior as the previous generation or become a new market of oldies for the leisure and tourism industry? However, to determine the actual number of senior citizens who will be travelling and to sought to evaluate and specify certain difficult to predict the actual numbers of senior citizen to any country. However, they can be based on the implicit assumption that there is a close relationship between the travel behavior of past, present and future seniors. But is this a valid assumption? As the revise- analysis travel analysis survey, which was conducted in Germany every year, offered some interesting data possibilities. It was designed to monitor the holiday travel behavior, opinions and attitudes of Germans and has been carried out since 1970 year, questions in the questionnaire. Data are based on face to face interviews, with a representative sample of more than 7,500 respondents, the interviews being carried out in January each year. All results refer to the average for the defined generated, which ranges generally over ten years. The group of people then at the age of 60 to 69 age is described. This corresponds to the same generation ten years ago, when they had an age of 50 to 59 age. When this methodological approach is not necessarily very sophisticated, it does have the important advantages of being cost effective.

IS (AI) big data gathering method a better psychological method to compare human marketing research method predict travel behavioral consumption?

On the psychological view point, I think individual traveler's character will have those kind of personal characteristics. First, simplicity searchers value above everything ease not transparency in their travel planning and holiday making, and are willing to avoid having to go through extensive research. Second, cultural purists use their travel as an opportunity to immerse themselves in an unfamiliar looking to break themselves entirely from their home lives and engage. Sincerely with a different way of living. Third, social capital seekers understand that to be well travelled is a personal quality, and their choices are shaped by their desire to take maximum of social reward from their travel. They will exploit the potential of digital media to enrich and inform their experiences, and structure their adventures always keeping in mind they are being watched by online audiences. Finally, reward hunters seek a return on the investment who make in their busy , high-achieving lives. Linked in part to the growing trend of wellness, including both physical and mental self-improvement who seek truly extraordinary and often indulgent or luxurious' must have experiences.

Why needs to know the personal character of individual traveler's characteristics? Because if travel agents could feel which kinds of individual traveler's character, then who can predict which kind of travel package to design to them more easily. For example, how to determine future travel behavior from past travel experience and perceptions of risk and safety? We need to concern that the influences of past international travel experience, types of risk associated with international travel and the overall degree of safety feeling during international travel on individual's travelling experiences likelihood of travelling to various geographic regions on their next international vacation trip or avoidance of those regions, due to perceived risk. Because individual traveler's experience of safety risk degree to the countries, it will influence who chooses to go to the countries/country to travel again.

Why travelers avoid certain destinations are as relevant decision making as why who choose to go to the country(countries) to travel. Perceptions of risk and safety and travel experiences are likely to influence travel decisions; efforts to predict future travel behavior can benefit to individual tourist's decision making.

As Weber & Bottern (1989) defined risky decision is as "choices among alternatives that can be described by probability distributions over possible outcomes" (p.114). Some psychologists judge subjective perceptions of physical reality, i.e. image of a particular tourist destination, whereas value judgement refers to the way individual rank destinations according to whose attributes. i.e. attractiveness, safety, risk etc. factors to form on overall image. So, if the individual traveler had unhappy and worried and unsafe experiences to go to where the place(country) to travel during whose vacation time before. Then, this negative travel experience will influence who is afraid to go to the place (country) to travel again. Risk of place, country, destination or region means the danger is relatively high to the place, i.e. increasing in airplane accidents, crime or terrorist activity targeting citizens of potential traveler's nationality or the probability of occurrence is great , i.e. recent occurrences involving travel regions/destinations under consideration or effective actions to control consequences exist. i.e. selecting safe regions and destinations, taking extra precautions when traveling to risky destinations. These risk factors will influence the individual traveler who chooses to cancel travel plan to go to the country again.

Another interesting research, how to predict behavioral intention of choosing a travel destination, which has focus of tourism research for years, but the complex decision making process leading to the choice of a travel destination has not been well researched. The planned behavior model using its core constructs, attitude, subjective norm and perceived behavioral control, with the addition of the past behavioral variable on behavioral intention of choosing a travel destination.

Understanding why people travel and what factors influence their behavioral intention of choosing a travel destination is beneficial to tourism planning and marketing. Understanding travel motivation is the push and pull model. The idea of the push and pull model is the decomposition of an individual's choice of a travel destination into two forces. The first force is the push factor that pushes an individual away home and attempts to develop a general desire to go somewhere else, without specifying where that may be. The second force is the pull factor, that pulls on individual toward a destination, due to a region specific travel location or perceived attractiveness of a destination. The respective push and pull factors illustrate that people travel because who are pushed by their internal motives and pulled by external forces of a destination. Nevertheless, how push and pull factors guide people's attitude and how these attributes lead to behavioral intentions of choosing a travel destination have rarely been investigated. The decision making process leading to the choice of a travel destination is a very complex process. The planned behavior model is as a research framework to predict the behavioral intention of choosing a travel destination. The model based on the three constructs of attitude, subjective norm, and perceived behavioral control (Fishbein & Ajzen, 1975).

In conclusion, the factors can influence travelers who decide to choose to travel the country, which include personal safety was perceived to the highest motivation factors among the important factors which include, scenic beauty, cultural interests, friendliness of local people, price of trip, services in hotels and restaurants, quality and variety of food and shopping facilities and services. The factors include both push and pull. Push factors include knowledge, prestige, and enhancement of human relationship etc., whereas, the most significant pull factors include high technologic image, expenditure and accessibility etc. For example, Japanese travelers visiting Hong Kong. Push factors are such as exploration dream fulfillment and pull factors are such as benefits sought, attractions and good climate city. It will be the factor of future travel patterns and motivations of sub-cultural and ethic groups for Japanese choice to go to Hong Kong travelling.

How can apply (AI) digital channel (big data gathering method) predict travelling consumer behaviors?

(AI) big data digital channel can be applied to help travelling businesses to evaluate whether how much the e-ticket price and travelling package price is the most attractive or reasonable to persuade travelling consumers feel it is the most reasonable price to choose to buy the airline's e-tickets or the travel agent's travelling package product from internet channel . It helps travelling consumers to feel which airlines or travelling agents which ought change their e-ticket and/or travelling package price to let travelling consumers to choose to buy the airline e-ticket or the travelling agent's travelling package products from internet channel. It can be applied to predict whether how many travelling consumer numbers can be increased or decreased when the airline e-ticket price is variable or the travelling agent travelling package price is variable . It aims to give opinions to help any online airlines or travelling agents to judge whether which e-ticket or travelling package price is the most reasonable to let travelling consumers to accept to choose to buy which airline's e-tickets or traveling agent's package products more attractive.

Thus, (AI) e-ticket or e-travelling package price measurement technology can be preference to be applied online communication ecommerce and mobile phone internet platform aspect. As traveling businesses can enter their past e-ticket or travelling package prices data and past travelling customer number data into computer or mobile. Then, (AI) price measurement technology can gather these data to analyze these e-ticket or travelling package product prices and past travelling customer number to compare their e-ticket and/or travelling package prices variable changing range level to find their e-ticket and /or travelling package price variable difference to measure to make conclusion about every travelling package or/and e-ticket product's price variable changing will influence how many travelling customer number increase or decrease changing to choose to sell their different kinds of travelling package or e-ticket products more accurate. Then, (AI) price measurement software will help them to analyze all past e-ticket and/or travelling package price variable changing data to compare whether which e-ticket and/or travelling package price range can let travelling customers to feel it is more reasonable and attractive to influence them to choose to buy their e-ticket or travelling package product among different airlines and travel agent choices. Because any e-ticket or travelling package product's price is one important factor to influence travelling consumers to choose to buy the airline's e-tickets or travelling agent's travelling package products.

For example, Amazon publish has applied (AI) price measurement technology to help authors to decide how much every different topic of e-book or paper book price, it can attract the largest number of readers to buy. Any one author only needs to type whose book name to Amazon publish author himself/herself Amazon website. Amazon publish (AI) price measurement learning machine will help them to auto-calculate and judge how much e-book or paper book price is the most attractive and the most reasonable in order to increase reader number to buy their e-books or paper books to read. So, (AI) online price measurement machine will gather past similar book names and past every similar book readers' reading times and the number of readers to give opinions to let every author to judge whether his/her very new e-book or paper book ought charge how much price to the e-book or paper book which can attract many readers to choose to buy. Although, it is not ensure that the e-book or paper book price must let readers to feel it is the most reasonable price to choose to buy in reader's view point. However, it has other factors to influence readers' choice to buy the e-book or paper book, e.g. whether the book content is attractive to public, the author's familiarity, the book's page is enough or not to satisfy readers to read etc. factors. But, instead of all these extra factors to influence readers to choose to buy the book to read. (AI) price measurement learning machine can real give opinions to every author to let them to judge the e-book or paper book different price range whether is too high to influence readers to choose to buy to read or tool low to influence readers feel it is possible poor content book to compare other similar content books. Thus, (AI) price measurement machine can help authors to predict every reader's reading behaviors or reading experience and reading habit from online channel in short time easily. The author only enter the book name to let Amazon publish price measurement machine to check, it will follow past reader's reading habit and reading experience to judge whether the similar all book topic sale record to judge how much price is the reasonable price to attract many readers to buy the book.

Hence, (AI) can be applied to digital channel to help travelling businesses to predict travelling consumer behavior in the future. In the future, mobile/smartphone, laptop, desktop will be most frequent used ecommerce channels to develop online business. So, (AI) can be also applied to these platforms to gather data to make analysis to help travelling businesses to predict travelling consumer purchase behaviors popularly. Due to , ecommerce is popular to global, so digital online and instore channels can be one good channel to let (AI) learning machine to make platform to gather past every online travelling consumer purchase (buying) experience data to help travelling businesses to build airline or travelling agent brand personality and having a responsible, positive impact on society.

To apply (AI) learning machine technology to understand travelling customer online purchase behavior, it will raise business e-commerce successful chance: For example, (AI) learning machine can help travelling businesses to gather data to analyze to determine whether short-term or long-term signals in the online travelling consumer behavior that indicate higher purchase intents to let every online travelling business to know. (AI) learning machine can find that online users with long-term purchasing intent tend to save and click through on more content.

However, as online travelling users approach the time of purchase their activity becomes more topically focused and actions shift from saves to searches from online travelling consumption channel. Then, (AI) learning machine will further find that the brand airline and/or travelling agent purchase signals in online travelling consumption behavior can exist weakness before an online travelling purchase is made and can also be traced across different online travelling purchase categories. Finally, (AI) learning machine synthesize these insights in predictive models of online travelling user purchasing intent to the brand of airline or/and travelling agent travelling package product. Taken together, it's work identifies a set of general principles and signals that can be used to model online travelling user e-ticket and/or travelling package purchasing intent across many online content discovery applications. Thus, (AI) learning machine can help online travelling businesses to gather any online travelling users' click online travelling behaviors data to judge whether there are how many online travelling users will choose to find their online travelling business websites to make final decisions to buy their travelling package or/and e-ticket products from online channels. Then, it will give opinions to help the online travelling businesses to let it to judge whether what are the important website factors will help its online travelling business to attract many online travelling consumers, e.g. designing unattractive travelling website issue, online unattractive scene photos issue, unclear website travelling photo color issue, unclear website travelling advertisement message, contents and words impressions issue, lacking image movement frequent attractive seeing issue etc. different website factors. Thus, online digital channel will be one good choice to apply (AI) learning machine to help travelling businesses to predict travelling consumer behaviors.

Thus, (AI) big data technology can also assist travelling consumers to gather different manufacturers' data to compare what their advantages and disadvantages of their travelling package products are. Then, travelling consumers can make comparison to choose which airline or travelling agent is the suitable to whom to buy e-ticket or pre-booking travelling package in online travelling consumption market.

.

Thus, I believe that artificial intelligent "big data" gathering method can be suggested to be applied to attempt to predict travelling consumer behavioral changes in global online travelling business environment, the reasons are as below:

On the travelling consumer's beneficial hand, travelling consumers can apply this (AI) big data gathering method to attempt to gather any global airline e-tickets and/or travelling agent's package product data to be analyzed by this artificial intelligent learning system to compare human general marketing research method, e.g. survey, questionnaire, marketing plan etc. different human judgement methods to predict traveler consumption behavioral change model. Then, it analyzed all the different data to compare what are the range of the most reasonable e-ticket and/or travelling package online purchase history and sale in order to make more accurate prediction to future traveler change traveling consumption behavioral model in next month, or next half year or next year short term period traveling consumption change prediction. Thus, it seems that future AI tool can be attempted to apply to predict any industries price behavior, e.g. deciding what level of price is the attractive level to attract consumer in these industries, e.g. fuel, education, tourism, health, entertainment, etc. different product purchase. It can give more absolute price suggestion to any merchants to set their price change predict in order to increase many customer numbers to buy their products in every year, or every quarter every month, or month week, even every day etc. different sale period.

Reference

Backman and others "motivation is conceptually viewed as " a state of need, a condition that services as a driving force to display different kind of behavior toward certain types of activities, developing preferences, arriving at some expected satisfactory outcome.", 1995, p.15.

Fishbein & Ajzen, "The model based on the three constructs of attitude, subjective norm, and perceived behavioral control". 1975.

Hsu et al. "A tourist behavior model has been developed, called the expectation, motivation and attitude " (EMA) model ,2010.

ICT,WWW . "Switzerland has one of the highest population-to-computer ratio in Europe." Switzerland, 2005.

Jorea Ministry of Environment, " For South Korea environmental attitude is a major factor in decision making vis-a-vis the consumption of " green" food and services", Korea, 2015.

Korea Ministry Of Environment. Public Organizations spend 2.2 Trillon Korean Won To
Purchase green Products in 2014; Ministry Of Environment: Sejoung, Korea, 2015.

Lind , Lohmann & Danielsson , United Nations Population Division, "Demographic change is said to be one of the important drivers for new trends in consumer traveling change behavior in most European countries". 2001.

Mayne, Lonnie. " Evolve of die in the age of the consumer". Entrepreneur, N.P. , 16 Apr. 2014. web of Oct. 2016.

Lee, D.; Kim, M. ; Lee, J. adoption of green electricity policies: Investigating the role of environmental attitudes via big data-driven search-queries. Energy policy 2016. 90, 187-201.

Lee, Terrence, " Tech in Asia-connecting Asia's startup system " Tech. in Asia- connecting Asia's startup ecosystem, N.p.,4 July 2016.

Weber & Bottorn "risky decision is as choices among alternatives that can be described by probability distributions over possible outcomes" , 1989, p.114.

CHAPTER V

Airport service improvement strategy

Any organizations will have life cycle stage from birth, growth , mature to decline. In airport service organizations have theis life cycle stages in service aspect. Airports organizatins aim to provide safe, comfortable , even shopping environment to let passengers to stay and to wait to transfer another air planes to visit another destination or arrive the country's airport to check out or check in to enter the airport to leave. If airports have life cycle stages, what the characteristics to every stage? How to improve airport service in order to reach mature life cycle stage rapidly? How to implement airport service strategy in order to reach mature life cycle stage to the aorport organization rapidly?I shall explain as below:

Any airports need to be planned in order to raise excellent service to let passengers to let any travelers choose to travel the country whether the country can provide excellent service and facilities. It will bring indirect emotion impact to influence the travelers chooce to revisit the country to travel again. However, soft or hard element or) staff service performance or airport facility), they will influence whether the different countries travelers to choose to travel to re-visit the country again. So, learning how to keep the mature or airport service life cycle stage to stay long time, it will be one important factor to influence any airport business in success.

In the birth life style stage to airport, airport organizations must maintain the capability to provide expert advice to airport owners an matters including operational safety, during construction, environmental compatibility, and airport development standards. No other private or public organization can be expected maintain this level of proficiency. These value-added services enhance public trust when assuring consistant application of standards for the nation's airport system. So, it seems that when the new airport is built if it hopes its passenger customers can consider themselves emotion need. So, it ought concentrate on nowadays airplane landing cunways or airport transfer free service transport etc. facilities can let them to feel safe when they were walking in any airport places. If they feel anywhere are dangerous when they are walking or staying in the ne sirport, then new airport non safe or dangerous factor may influence travelers to choose the country to travel again.

Any new airports will need have good new national airport plan in order to it might operate in the near future with respect to safety areas. The plan elements may include as below:

Achieving zero accidents aim, establish standard safety areas at all commercial service airports , achieving the most minimum 85% of all passenger flights operate on runways with safe feeling, increase measure to 100% of all passenger flight operating on runways with standard safety areas after three months. Within 5 years, 95% of all passenger flights begin and end on runways with standard safety areas.

On benefits aspect, aims to mobilize work force to improve safety area performance describes realistic investment benefits. So, in any new airports birth life cycle stage, they must need to consider safety and expenditure for repair aspect in order to keep its service performance to avoid passengers have dissatisfactory feeling when they are staying in their new airports.

When the country has many travelers travel to the country , then the country's new airport passengers number must increase. It is its the new airport growth life cycle stage. These are critical success factors influence the airport, whether it can improve service performance in order to excite different countries travelers visiting the country's airport desire or grow up the visitors number successfully. The critical success factors may include: Having necessary support from internal and externa stakeholders to implement and willing to share information and identify anywhere the total airport facilities of repair needs that are both reliable and feasible projections to let passengers to feel more safe feeling when they are staying in the airport, understand its future service vision and mission, set strategic direction and goals to process/product specific objectives and decision-making across and doen the organization, define, model and prioritize planning prcesses critical for mission performance, practice hand-on sernior management ownership of planning process and allow field, personnel flexiblity in performing jobs, adjust organizational structures , an essessment program to evaluate planning process and product management , e.g. national airport system performance, create organizational understanding of the value management to customer and stakeholder current and future expectations developing human resources management strategies to support new process that solves needs planners and engineers, building information resources strategies change, especially for entering data at the source and maintains data integrity and timeliness.,establish central support group to support reengineering efforts, outreach and training efforts across the organization, phase in short-and long-term results that achieve set goals and objectives over the next two years.

Thus, when one new airport begins to feel passengers number is increasing. It ought experience the growth life cycle stage to the new airport , if it hopes that it can reach mature life cycle stage rapidly as well as keeps its mature life cycle stage to stay in this stage long time or reachs the airport service performance to the most satisfactory level in this mature life cycle stage. It must need to attempt to plan these strategies to implement in order to avoid decline life cycle stage occurs in short time. So, it explains why some new airport can experience the development to mature life cycle stage from grow life cycle stage in short time,even when it reachs mature life cycle stage. It can keep to stay in this stage long time. The reason is that it had prepared effective strategies to achieve how to improve its airport service performance aim in order to satisfy passenger needs. When they are staying in the country's airport any time. Hence, every year revising service performance is needed to any airports.

Any airports must have development processes. The question is that whether the airport needs how long time to reach growth or mature life cycle stage from birth stage or decline life cycle stage will be delayed how long to occur. The development processes may mean that the airport development life cycle stages changes that had toard a particular result or even as a series of continuous actions or operations coducting to an end (Merriam-Webster, 2013).

reference

Merriam-webster (2013). On line dictionary. Available at:

https://www.merriam-webster. com/(last accessed July , 8 2013).

Hence, any airport organizations with experience development pricess. When the new airport is built, it must be in the birth life cycle stage. Its passengers number can not increase rapidly. It needs time to grow their number. But, when the new airport operates a period, many different countries begin feel this new airport is existence in the country. They will attempt to catch airplance to visit this country airport to catch airplane to visit tis country airport to travel. If they feel this country airport service performance can satisfy their short time staying feeling or its passengers or airports visitors number may increase rapidly. It meand that this airport is experiencing growth life cycle stage. So, if the airport can attract many visitors in short time. It will reduce time to growth life cycle stage from birth life cycke stage.

So , service performance may be one important factor to inflow the airport grows. When the airport develops to the period, passengers number can not increase rapidly, it may be the airport's mature life cycle stage. Due to it's passengers number can not grow rapidly, its passengers number also may reduce. When its passengers number has significant decrease, if its reduction number is increasing more. It implies that the airport is experiencing decline life cycle stage. All any country's airport may experience whole life cycle stages. If the country's airport can not implement successful strategies, it may experience birht life cycle stage in long time because it can not grow its passengers number significantly. So, any airports need to learn how to help them to change growth life cycle stage, even mature life cycle stage can stay in long time easily. If they hope to attract many different countries passengers to visit their airports or travel themselves countries or enjoy to stay short time in themselves airports in order to grow themselves airline industry development.

● How can processes improvement management strategy influence airport service performance?

Overall processes in an airport may involve passengers, luggage, cargo, aircraft movements, ground handling, and crews . All of these operations can be systematised into processes at airport terminal. Three main types of processes can be established departing , arrival and transfer . Departure consists in catching a flight to a final or intermediate destination, arrival consists in landing and leaving the airport, and transfer consists in landing at the airport only to catch another flight to a final or an intermediate destination. Airports also deal with cargo. It involves in the movement of cargo by air, cargo fies from the shopper to the consignee through one or more airlines. However, when the airport can let them freight forwarder, being familiar with the necessary procedures how permits the airline to concentrate on the provision of air transport and to avoid time consuming details of the facilitation and landside distribution system. It will raise efficiency and improve service performance. The services product by the ground handling are crucial to the success and efficiency of the airport operations.

These services are usually provided by specialised companies. Briefly, it includes the luggage treatment, passengers carrying from plan to terminal when needed and aircraft assistance. Also, focusing on crew, there are two majoe processes, one for departures and the other for arrivals. The crew members also have to pass the security and passport controls. However, they have special channels for this. Once they reach the aircraft, the similarities with the passengers' procedure stop. Hence, they have to perform a set of activities , such as check the aircraft load sheets and help passengers to name a few. Also airport terminal operations processes for passengers and luggage, typically for departures , passengers do the check on the airline area, pass security controls, proceed to the general lounge and lastly to the gate holding area. arriving passengers are able to immediately go from the luggage claim area, but the non-passengers have to pass the passport control at first. After this passengers have to decide if they need to declare goods or not as the paths are different . Hence, if the airport can reduce all of this service processes are less complex as immigration check in-out service, liggage claim can be efficient to carry when passengers need to find themselves luggage. Then, it will reduce waste time and let they satisfy airport service absolutely. So, reducing service process time amy also help the airport to increase customers number significantly. When airport role is the middleman between airlines , cargo transport service providers and passengers, e.g. short time transport cargo service and reducing passengers check in or check out service time. then, it will let them to feel more satisfactory service to the airport.

Hence, airport capacity is as a multifactor function leaves open the exact relationship between the factors but stresses that all factors are relevant to assess airport capacity . So , understanding airport capacity and what drives the capacity usage at airports may provide an insight in the set of instructments available to optimise the use of capacity. All of these factors may influence any capacity of an airport, they may include as below:

For example, technical constraints, e.g. ATM per hour service in a runway in a combined arrival and departure fashion, when many passengers are staying at the airport, they can withdraw money from ATM easily. So, ATM number facilities service supply number and location choice to the airport factors will infuence passengers ' satisfactory level, another factor is environmental constraints, it can directly offer the wellbeing of the communities surrounding the negative emotion to passengers and communities surrounding the airprt. For this factor, the change in technology and/or operational procedures can provide more capacity in the system.

Airline business models factor, it can affect the capacity spoke model when other under a point-point one ,these models directly affect the peak hour operational capacity, particularly in big international hubs. Airlines often compete with high frequencies between destinations, thus increasing the number of movements. In addition, conncectivity also has downsides for this model: the delays in one airport might be exported and sometimes in another, due to the connectivity influencing the real capacity. This factor has been setting economic incentives or pricing models. Furthermore, expanding information systems, from one airport to multiple airports gate-to-gate concept, and the use of larger airport to redcuce frequencies.

Hence, above these factors may influence whether the airport needs how long time to reach maturiry life cycle stage when it is staying the growth life cycle stage. It depends on how its strategies implementation and how environment influence its implementation , if it hopes to achieve to reach the maturity life cycle stage in success in short time.

Finally, I shall explain life cycle cst analysis to any country pavement strategy will bring what significant influential benefits to any airports continue to develop in order to avoid to reach decline life cycle stage time in short time easily , when they are staying in the mature life cycle stage. In the construction or rehabilitation investments of highway's pavements, it is already common to perform a life-cycle analysis or life cycle cost analysis for different alternatives to airport pavements. Becauae when any airport pavements are using for a long time, every day has many airplanes need to fly to land on the pavement. It can bring significant repace influence when the airport has many airplanes are needed to land on the pavements every day in the maturity life cycle stages.

Hence, how to evaluate the repair cost expenditure budget in order to satisfy every day air planes land on the airport pavement need. In the calculations are different cost factors (including direct and indirect cost)to any airport itself pavement. Direct costs are related to the critical construction cost landing on pavement activities and are calculated with information from the airport agency and constructors that work for them. The indirect costs are related with the loss of daily revenue of the airport during work activities, such as landing on the airport pavement.

Runways are the most critical pavements area of airport , so it is critical to ensure the quality of these pavement to let airplanes to land on the airport safety, e.g. they need to be constructed with sufficient strength to carry the moving airport and have a high resistance to skidding and aquaplaining. It is most of the time accomplished with reconstructions or deep rehabilitation. Hence, predicting how much will spend on airport pavement facilities expenditure must need in every day.

However, the life cycle assessment (LCA) is a mult step procedure for calculating the life time environmental impact of a product or service is needed to any airport organizations, when they reachs maturity life cycelt stage . The complex process includes goal and cope definition in inventory analysis impact assessment. The process is vaturally iterative as quality and completeness of information is constantly being testes. When the definition of the aim and scope of the study is done the next step is the development of an inventory, in which all significant environmental burdens during the lifetime of the product,, such as airport pavements or process , such as airplanes landing on the pavement or airplanes leaving from the pavement in the airport.

(Araujo, Oliveria & Silve) 2014 explained that life cycle snslysis of pavements are focused on the activities of extraction, production, transportation application of materials, concisely the construction of the road. Because its difficult to obtain other relevant data knowing that the use phase of the pavement is predominant with repect to energy consumption and also to gas emissions related to the atmosphere. One of the main factors for the use phase is the rolling resistance, this depends on the surface and structural characteristics of the different pavements.

reference

Araujo, J.P.C. Oliveria, J.R.M. & Silva H.M.R.D. (2011) . the importance of the use phase on the LCA of environmentally friendly solutions for asphalt road pavements. transportation research part D: trasport and environment, 32(0), 97-110. Retrieved in March 2015 from://
dx. doi.org/10.1016/j.trd.2014.07.006.

Hence, , if the airport can have good repairment or renew skills to help its pavement to improve. Then, it may bring long time benefit, such as reducing airplanes energy consumption and also to avoid gas emissions or reduce gas emissions accident occurrene, even air plane landing on pavement accident occurrence chance can reduce to the zero. so, defining the expected pavement performance time improvement strategy can influence whether the airport pavement can satisfy all airplane users how long time landing on or leaving on the airport pavement. Also it is the major factor to influence airport main function success for any airplanes arriving to the country's airport pavement or leaving from the country's airport pavement. Hence, calculating any airport pavement life cycle costs factor. It is necessary to analysis and interpret carefully the results to identfy the most economic pavement strategy in any airport's whole life cycle development stages.

CHAPTER VI

Organizational decision making strategy

Every company must have strategy to make any important or not important decision. Any decisions must be very important because they may influence any companies' future development. So, our company management can not neglect to cosider whether all strategies are reasonable to influence any organizations success. However, we need to consider how to achieve effective decisions to avoid wrong decisions to cause our companies' development in long term.

The question is how to implement effective decision making to achieve every consequence to gain the best benefits to any organizations? Any organization managers ought need to follow these steps in order to make effective decisions. Acknowledge and compensate for your biases, use positive and negative lists, experiment by reversing your live of thinkin, create a scoring system. Any organizational decisions have four decision making styles. They may include these four basic categories for decion making, these being: Directive, conceptual, consultative, and consensue. So, strategic decisions usually mean managers must plan for change and risk.

Many factors are unknown, since managers are planning for future changes. Another example for a major change is the decision to modify the company's culture. For instance, the firm may be having trouble with increased employee turnover. It may be the company's culture needs to be changed in order to employees can adapt to work together. Hence, when one company's working environment and employees attidude is poor, because they feel unhappy to work, so working environment will be caused poor. It may be influenced whole organizational culture to be more poor. Hence, the organizational ought need to change its organizational culture to be more happy in order to let whole organization's employees can feel happy to work in this enjoyable working environment . Hence, any entrepreneurs or managers ought need to consider employees' emotion issue how to let they have good working emotion to do their tasks every day, e.g. get comfortable with the cost of deciding , teaching employees hoe to control themselves emotion, understand that logical decisions have a secret emotional intuitive is one of the simplest, and arguably one of the most common ways to make a decision, rational decision making is the type of decision making many people want to believe what they do.

The first stage model to any making strategic decisions, they may include: defining the problem, consider these questions, gathering information, seeking information on how any why the problem occurred, developing and evaluating options, generating a wide range of options, choosing the best action, selecting the option that best meets the decision objective. Hence, decision including strategies are the ways, we use information to make a choice, in this case, managers need to make strategic choices as muually exclusive options, start with the most apparent options, generate alteratives, specify the conditions under which each option is attractive, identify barriers to each option, design and run tests to prove or disprove each of the conditions, finally using the data, make a decision. Hence, business leaders use strategic decision-making when they plan the company's future strategic management involves definingl long term goals, responding to market forces and carrying out the firm's mission, so making strategic decisions managers look at the big picture.

In psychology view, decision making is regarded as the cognitive process , knowledge necessary to know when to use any strategies. They do posses to change their approach to decision making. Rather, think of it is a decision making process that keeps you from making the same mistakes year after year. Making-judgement-based decisions among a variety of variable options is made easier when a systematic process is utilized. So, decision making strategies are the structured method and operational guidelines followed by decision makers. So, any strategic decision making process is needed in the procedural rationality stage, if the organization expects to do the most reasonable decision making to solve any challenges. So, strategic decision making is essential on how top managers use process and tools to implement long-term goals. Also, decision making is a process that reduces uncertainty to a considerable level.

In most decisions, uncertainty will be reduced, when the manager had prepared one good strategic decision making method, the most difficult decison making suitation is that when the manager needs to implement a multiperspective strategic decision making. It is the process of making long-term decision's that helps or helps the organization t build long term benefits. However, any organization's managers ought need to spend time to learn a large variety of decision making techniques, it can help improve decisions of different types.

It can be useful in decision between strategies or investment opportunities with constrained resources. This is called strategic decision making, where decisions are made according to a company's goals or mission. At many organizations, it is up to managers to make the key decisions that influence business strategy. So, managers must need to learn how to implement any kinds of strategic decision making method in order to help their organizations to achieve the most reasonable long term benefits. However, with any strategic planning process, any organization will be able to know. What it wants to achieve in the long term vision is on ongoing process that involves crafting strategies to achieve goals.

● Why do managers feel difficult to make decisions?

Usually these factors may cause managers feel difficult to make decision for their organizations: Making decisions will always be difficult because it takes time and energy to weigh their options. Things like second-guessing the manager himself/herself and feeling indecisive and just a part of the process. However, decision-making is important to achieve the organizational goals/objectives within given time and budget. It searches the best alternative, utilizes the resources properly and satisfies the employees at the workplace. As a result, organizational goals or objectives can be achieved as per the desired result. Moreover, decision-making is an integral part of modern management.

Decisions play important roles as they determine both organizational and mangerial activities. A decision can be defined as a consequence of action purposely chosen from a set of alternatives to achieve organizational or managerial objectives or goals. The first step to making those decision is understanding what makes managers themselves so hard, the decisions that may include senior leaders, middle managers, frontline staffs , they many face short time or long time decision making challenge , when they need to find solution methods to solve any organizational challenges. For example, one manager needs to make decision to resolve organizational challenge before tomorrow morning time. Then, time pressure can lead to poor decision making to influence the manager feels physically, mentally ad personally pressure. He will have much chance to make poor decisions when he feels he is in a position of power. IF he can not make any decisions to help his organization to solve challenge before tomorrow morning, he will not achieve any satisfactory management effort to the company's senior management, even CEO . So, time pressure may be one main factor to cause the manager to do poor decision making to help his organization to solve the challenge.

So, if the manager hopes to make better decision making , he needs likely feel comfortable and confident making decisions, e.g. learning how to manage his senior manager or CEO expectations. However, some decisions carry enough weight that the prospect of simply making a choice can be made in short time. SO, the manager ought need to learn how to weight whether which choices may bring more benefits or advantages ro make any decision in short time frequently every day. It can train that when the manager encounter difficult problem to be solved in short time. He can be trained to judge whether which is the most suitable choice easily to do any decision more easily. So, daily learning how to solve any short time or long time decision making skill frequently, this learning behavior must help any managers to raise short time critical thinking decision making skilful effort. Hence, learning managing uncertainty and making the most reasonable choices , strategic decision making skill, it will be any organizational managers ought need to consider issue if they want to be the best strategic decision maker in themselves organizations.

Hence, any organizational managers need to know that decision making is difficult to taugh, particularly when there may not be one right answer. It's common for managers and leaders to feel alone. Being alone as a decision maker comes with the job. However, decision making is absolute one of the toughest parts of running a business. They will feel responsible for it, compared to the management announcing the change in policy without listening to what. Hence, self confidence, time management factor, is a important part to influence any managers to do any important decision making more success. So, they can not neglect how to train themselves to attempt to find the most reasonable decision making to solve any chalenges for themselves organizations in order to achieve one strategic decision maker for their organizations.

On conclusion, managers' attitudes toward work and incentives may influence his decision making whether it can be more accurate, when reviewing upon motivation, incentives, the social psychology of work and behavior at work, it is tempting to conclude that managers are motivated when manual workers need bonus payment, between ideas , beliefs attitudes. So, any managers individual personal attitudes will influence their behaviors, also his behaviors will motivate how he can make resonable decision making. So, manager's working attitude can be one factor to influence whether his/her decision making can be made more reasonable for his/her organization.

Computer technologic firm merger cooperational strategy

● IBM and Apple merger strategic advantages and disadvantages

IBM and Apple computer firms, they merger to cooperate together, whether merger will help them to bring what advantages and disadvantages ? What is the life cycle stage to these two big computer organizations? These two computer companies IBM and Apple , they had set up abut forty years. From 1970 year, when Apple founders, they had invented new computer machine to bring human playing electronic game to entertain at home. Then, IBM founder also invented micro softword clerical software to let any office workers or students or home users can type on computers to replace typing machines . So, Micro soft word software invention also help office workers or students or home users to choose to apply computer to do typing tasks to replace traditional typing machines. So, these two firms' borth stage, is that when Apple desktop computer products are innovated as well as Microsoft IBM micro soft word softwares are also innovated to this traditional typing market.

When, 1980, there are not that Microsoft word softare functions are, so these two founders will spend long time to promote desktop computers and microsoft word software new products to let many people know what their real functions are, e.g. playing electronic entertainment game activities and clerical tasks , these two main functions to let them to know, when they may be known whether what microsoft word software and Apple brand desktop computer can help any students or clerical office workers or home users to do any clerical tasks or play electronic playing game leisure activites at homes or offices. Then , many people begin to accept these both new products to use for their daily clerical tasks or electronic playing game lesiures activies .

However, in their birth life cycle stage time needs about two years short time only, because their advesrtisement strategies are effective to let global many people feel computer product can belp us to fo any clerical tasks or bring exciting electronic playing game leisure feeling when students feel bore, they may spend some times to apply computer to play any games at homes. Even they may turn on computers to apply Microsoft word sofware to help them to do any homeworks or assignments. Students can use computers to replace typing machines to type any clerical documents at homes or schools conveniently.

After1982 year, global IBM computer and Microsoft word software buyers number had been increasing rapidly. So, from 1982 year, these two firms are experiencing life style growing stage period. Till to 1988 year, these two firms may ensure global computer and software products main suppliers their computer and software technological products had high market share. So, in global computer and software technological market, these are not many competitors to win them. So, they do not need long time to enter life cycle growing stage. They only need four ro five years time to attract many global computer and software buyers begun to accept their products and also choose to buy their IBM and Microsoft computers and softwares to use.

Hence, then 1988 year, these two high technolgical computer and software product firms had been experiencing life cycle mature stage till to 2000. Although, in this forty , IBM and Apple computer firms number had been increasing rapidly globally. But, other computer and software competitors number is also increasing, e.g. Dell computer brand had be familiar to global computer buyers. Dell's market share is also high. So, their computer and software buyers may have many kinds of computers and softwares brands of product choices in global students and office clerical workers and home users computer and software product market.

In fact, IBM and Apple began to enter life cycle decline stage , due to laptop products need increase and many different brands of laptop computers may be supplied to let computer users to choose to buy in global computer market. So, after 2000 , these two computer firms began to change to new technologial product or service market, e.g. apply also invented Smart mobile products because it felt desktop and laptop products competitors number had been decreasing , due to they had many laptops and desktops competitors' products to choose to buy. So, Apple brand computer begun to invent smart mobile phone and small flat laptop , it has or has none phone function products in order to earn high market share to smart mobile and flat laptop product user market ratio in order to avoid life cycle decline stage reachs rapidly.

In fact, IBM smart mobile strategy may be effective to absord global some smart mobile customers. But IBM is skill desktop same smart mobile competitors. Also, IBM laptop and desktop products may also face different similar computer function products to choose from competitors.So, IBM will may enter life cycle decline stage rapidly. Also, Microsoft brand computer may be its main competitor, Microsoft can attempt to apply interest technology to help it to sell electronic book, because it felt desktop and laptop product market has reached mature stage.

It is common that global every family had own at least one laptop or desktop or both computer product. So, it means that product needers number begins to decrease, when global every family own at least one computer product to use at home, even global every office also wn at least one computer in offices. Unless, their computers are broken , thwy ill feel need to buy another new. Otherwise, they use computers about three to five years when they feel too old,then they will choose to change another new. So, Microsoft applies internet to help it to sell electronic book, it can bring another electconic publish business chance, instead of selling laptop, desktop, Microsoft software products only, because it also feel that when computer market had reached mature period. Global many people had owned computers, their needs will also decrease. Since internet invention, it creates e-commerce chance, electronic publishing is also popular to let global readers to read any books from desktop or laptop computers or mobile computers tools anywhere. So, Microsoft is attempting to enter this electronic publish market . this electronid publishing reading service market does not need readers to buy paper books to read, they won't need feel heavy if they need to bring bags to carry many heavy books to go to schools, libraries , students only need to bring laptops to read any Microsoft publish electonic books from computers anywhere conveniently. So, Microsoft electronic book pubishing new market help it to avoid to experience the life cycle decline stage rapidly. But, these two firms are still main competitors , if they choose not to merger or coopeerate to do technologic product, e.g. laptop, desktop , software or electronic book publish online reading service together. They may influence their clients number to reduce. Otherwise, if they can merger or cooperate , then it is possible that their clients nu,ber may increase or profit increase, even fight other computer and software companies competitors easily. Then, their computer and softare market share may raise when other competitors number reduces, e.g. Dell may be their main computer competitor, but if they cooperate or merger , then Dell's clients may be influenced to choose to buy their any desktops, laptops, softwares products. They can help themselves invention high technological products , if they can attribute their unique computer technology to help to invent any new kinds of more advanced computers or softwares , e.g. even high technological electronic reading platform to be improved to publish high reading quality of electronic books to attract many readers to read their electronic books from their publishing webstores.

IBM and Microsoft merger or cooperation can help them to raise market share or fight competitors in this often changing high technological computer product market. What are the disadvantages and advantges when they choose to merger or cooperate together? I shall explain as below:

Can IBM and Microsoft merger can keep their computer , software , even electronic book publish market in the mature life cycle stage in long time in order to avoid decline life cycle stage occurs. IBM's global strategy is based on three aspects: cloud , data and engagement . IBM's strategy imperatives may is business growth on cloud, analytics, mobile, social and society . So, it has changed its old strategy only concentrates on computer sold aspect. Since internet technology had been invented. However, IBM's primary generic strategy is cost leadership.

In Michael Porter's model, the generic strategies are what companies use to ensure competitive advantages . The cost leadership generic competitive strategy supports IBM's competitive advantages through cost-effectiveness of its operaton. However, if IBM can operate or merger to Microsoft, then Microsoft ought may help it to reduce more cost , when their technology can assist to develop their products, e.g. IBM's clouds , data technologic strengths can be brought to Microsoft 's product or Microsoft's electronic book publishing technology or software manufacturing technology strengths can bring to IBM' s products to assist themselves to raise computer, smartphone phoe, electronic publishing reading technological service business competitive effort in global computer , smartphone and electronic book publish markets. Then, when IBM can own Microoft 's technology , it may help it to reduce manufacturing cost in possible.

In fact, instead of IBM may merger to microsoft to reduce its cost to be more. It may also merger to Amazon, Amazon is us one online electronic book sale provider, it help global different businesses to apply itself online platform to sell their products. It is middleman role, it helps any sellers to sell their products from its online store platform. Any one can turn on computer and click to Amazon website to buy any products . Amazon will help any buyers to deliver their products to their homes by flight , after they pay visa card, because Amazon is global the topest online product sale service middleman provider. It's cloud technology is very proficient. If Amazon and IBM can merger to cooperate to do themselvers cloud service high technological business. IBM can apply Amazon's cloud high technological platform to help itself to grow its business and increase its cloud service clients number more easily. So, IBM ought choose Amazon's cloud platform to assist itself to continue to develop its future cloud service business, e.g. electronic book publish, because Amazon's electronic book publish market has have high reading market share.

Hence, IBM needs to find, e.g. Amazon or Microsoft to expand its high technological product or cloud strategy or cloud technology may be IBM's main competitors. If Amazon and IBM and Microsoft can merger or cooperate to expand themselves unique computers or softwares ot smart mobiles or electronic book platform sale markets to be merger together, then global computer buyers , smart mobiles buyers , electronic book readers, electronic platform product buyers must may enjoy the most benefits, because they can attribute their unique computers, smart mobiles manufacture, cloud service platform technology to be applied to themselves unique computers, smart mobiles, electronic book reading flatform and ebooks ale mix together, t means to improve these products or services unique function or improve themselves technology in order to let global computer , smart mobile or electronic book readers or electron platform product buyers feel that their these products or cloud platform products sale or reading service performance can br improved. Hence, their merger ought bring advandages more than disadvantages.

However , I shall also indicate some possible disadvantages to IBM merger strategy. Higher prices to IBM products, A merger can reduce competition and give the IBM more monopoly power with less competition and greater market share to IBM, but when IBM chooses to merger to Micrsoft and / or IBM chooses to merger to MIcrosoft and/ or Amazon , they may influence IBM's computer or smartmobile phone products can usually increase prices for consumers. Then, consumers may also compare IBM's products to other computer and smart mobile phone sellers. If they feel its price is not reasonable, they may choose to buy other smart mobiles or choose to buy other brands of laptops, desktops to replace IBM's product. Because IBM's any products prices may be controlled or dominated by Microsoft or Amazon after they merger. So, IBM can not change itself products prices more easily. It is its weaknesses . Another risk's associated with mergers and acquisitions to IBM, it may be differences in culture between Amazon and Microsoft and IBM. It may bring inefficient communication and lack of transparency to IBM organization when Amazon and Microsoft staffs may participate to IBM any important decisions. It may bring miscalculations in the evaluation of assets to IBM. For example, merger may bring disadvantages when the main drivers behind the Lenovo and IBM merger. The drivers behind the merger between China's Lenovo and US IBM was inspired by several moves. The main one being the loss that the latter incurred to IBM itself pc division after a change of business strategy.

On conclusion , before IBM decides to implement merger strategy to any technological firms, it needs to consider whether what risks they may bring and what benefit they may bring after IBM itself chooses to merger to the firm in order to avoid miscalculation consequence to influence IBM's business continues to develop or reachs life cycle decline stage rapidly.

CHAPTER VII

Oil industry users strategy

● Reasons cause oil industry experiences
decline life cycle stage
Nowadays, global oil industry is experiencing decline cycle stage. From 1950 oil energy product is at the birth cycle stage. When cars , human walking replace tool is invented, human began to drive cars to go to anywhere in habit daily. Because human is often to drive cars to go to offices, or leisure places, so cars can cause gas need increases. Before, 1970, oil energy product is at the growth cycle stage, becuse cars are accepted to Western people more than Asia people only. But, after 1970, in Asia many countries, e.g. China, Japan, Singapore etc. people began to accept cars to replace catching public transport tools, so gas need had been increasing . Till to 1990. oil industy had been experiencing mature life cycle stage, because global car manufacture number had increased, global every family may have at least one car when the parent has children. So, global cars need number increases, it may be one factor to bring gas need increases. Also global travelers number increases, it will cause many airplanes need to fly to different countries frequently. So, it also bring gas need increases. Because global drivers and travelers number increases, this factor may cause gas need increases significantly because driving activities and flying activities are frequently occurence. However, nowadays oil industry is experiencing decline cycle life stage. Because COVID-19 human mouth disease influences many travelers feel fear to catch air planes when they need to sit in closed window airplanes , if one passenger has COVID 19 disease, he/she will bring other passengers to get this kind of lung disease by air contact. So, global travelers number decreases, it can influence airplanes need to fly frequently, so gas need is also influenced to reduce. Also, since electronic vehicle invention, because electronic vehicle is charged battery for its energy, so gas does not absolute need. If global many drivers have environmental protection awareness, they choose to buy electronic vehicles to replace traditional gas vehicles, then gas need must be influenced to decrease. So, these two main factors may influence global oil industry need decrease. The question is that: How gas manufacturers raise gas users need from decline life cycle stage to re-grow life cycle stage? I shall indicate the methods as below:

   ● How to raise global gas users need desire ?
Future of sustainable resources
scarcity economic and social loss to oil industry

In economic theory, it indicates two major factors are responsible for the emergence of economic problems. They are (i) the existence of unlimited human wants and (ii) the scarcity of available resources, such as limited numbers of food and natural resource shortage. I feel that human need to solve these two problems before 2050 years. How to balance an optimization approach for human and ecological flow needs ? How to solve climate change environment problem and welfare is for the centrality of human need? Because natural environment factor and natural resource and food shortage and our social economic growth which will have close connection relationship. If natural environment is bad, it will influence a lot of crops numbers can't be grown in farms. The reason of crops shortage will be caused, due to numbers of crops supply to be reduced because bad weather can not grow much crops and overpopulation numbers will increase largely at the same time before 2050 year. It will cause the numbers of demand is more than supply seriously. The result of the prices of foods will be increased by overpopulation and food shortage, so that it will cause every country inflation will be risen, it will occur in developing countries urban areas due to which have , such as India , China, Africa etc. countries have no many farms to provide to farmers to grow foods because air and water pollution and factories are built on farm land , so which need to pay higher price to import crops and foods to provide whose overpopulation to eat from overseas developed countries. Experience of developing countries that have succeeded in the reducing hunger and malnutrition shows that economic growth doesn't automatically ensure success, the source of growth matters too. This isn't surprising since 75% of the poor in developing countries live in rural areas and their incomes are directly or indirectly linked to agriculture. Many countries will continue depending on international trade to ensure their food security. It is estimated that by 2050 year developing countries net import of rice will were than double from 135 million tones in 2008/2009 to 300 million in 2050 year. It seems overpopulation will cause developing countries foods shortages in 2050 years.

Climate change and increased biofuel production represent major risks for long term food security. Studies estimate that the aggregate negative impact of climate change on African agricultural output up to 2080 year to 2100 year could be between 15% and 30%. Agriculture will have to adapt to climate change, but it can also help mitigate the effects of climate change. A recent study estimates that continued rapid expansion of biofuel production up to 2050 year would lead to the number of pre-school children in Africa and South Asia being 3 and 1.7 million higher. Thus, policies promoting the use of food based biofuels need to be reconsidered with the aim of reducing the competition between food and fuel for scare resources. The sharp increases in food price that occurred in global and national markets in recent years, and the resulting increases in the number of hungry have sharpened the awareness of policy makers and of the general public. Hence, different countries governments need to concern safe agricultural system to avoid any foods shortage to supply after 2050 year.

The perspective for 2050 year raises a number of important questions. Are current public and private investments sufficient to ensure adequate agricultural production potential, sustainable use of natural resources, information and communication research for technological breakthroughs to avoid foods shortage for the future? What needs to be undertaken to help agricultural meet the challenges of climate change and growing energy scarcity? What can be done to ensure food security in Africa, India , China etc. developing countries. The facing highest population growth rates,. The severest impacts from climate change and the heaviest burden of HIV/AIDS etc. diseases threats.

Finally, on the changing socio-economic environment hand, the main socio-economic factors that drive increasing food demand are population growth, increasing urbanization and rising incomes. In 2007 year, the USA dept. of Economic and Social affairs indicated that in fact, the developed countries population growth is slower than developing countries. However, all of the growth in the world's population will take place in urban areas. By 2050 year, more than 70% of the world's population is expected to be urban. Thus, scientists need to concern to predict developing countries urban area people foods demand and supply both numbers whether global foods can provide enough supply to urban area people in developing countries after 2050 year. On the other side, human will concern whether there be enough natural resource base of land, water and genetic diversity to meet developing countries needs after 2050 year.

What factors cause the resources scarcity and why human need to solve the resources scarcity before 2050 year

In comparison to the past 50 years, the rate at which pressure are building up on natural resources-land, water, bio-diversity will be increasing during the coming 50 years. An expanded use of agricultural feedstock for biofuels and ongoing environment degradation would work in the opposite direction. Much of the natural resource base already in use worldwide shows degradation . These include capture fisheries and water supply . In addition, actions to other ecosystem services, such as the ecosystem service, food production often cause the degradation of others, soil nutrient depletion, erosion, desertification, deflection of freshwater reserves, loss of tropical forest and biodiversity are clear indicators.

Whether natural resource base should be adequate to meet the future demand at global level. Whether any developing countries should still limit commercial natural resource import capacity to let rural area population to use to protect whose domestic natural industry development when rural area population will be increasing seriously in 2050 year. Biodiversity, another essential resource for agricultural and food production is threatened by urbanization , deforestation, pollution and the conversion of wetlands. As a result of agricultural modernization, changes in diets and population density, humankind increasingly depends on a reduced amount to agricultural biological diversity for its food supplies.Thus major reforms and investments are needed in all regions to cope with rising scarcity and degradation of land, water and biodiversity and with the added pressures resulting form rising incomes, climate change and energy demands.

There is a need to establish the right incentives to protect agriculture's environmental services to protect biodiversity and to ensure food production using new agricultural technologies before 2050 year. For the developing countries, in order to ensure that resources are available in the required quantity and quality and in the urban locations where they are needed, large additional investments need to be made in order to avoid rural people of hunger coincides with resource scarcity before 2050 year. Increased investment incentives and provided stable production growth incentives : land, water and biodiversity of three natural resources. The aim should be to stop over-exploitation, degradation and pollution, promote efficiency gains and expand overall capacities as appropriate . To provide the rural population engaging in ecosystem services with win-win solution to improve the sustainability of ecosystems, mitigate climate change and improve rural incomes. Whether and under what conditions the estimated future food demand can be met and how food security can be achieved. Hence, every country needs to have an effective economy system to attempt to solve the basic economic problems. The function of the economy is to allocate scarce resources among unlimited wants. Moreover, every country needs to have effective economic system to study of its citizen behavior in relation to how scarce resources to allocated and how choices are made between alternative uses of the country government's limited expenditure. Due to our earth has scarce resources, it implies human will scarce natural resources to provide us to use. Our governments need to predict whether what our earth's limited natural resources will be all used in order to solve our natural resources to be used in the short time quickly as well as our governments need to apply effective economic system to design soluble methods to avoid our earth will be not to provide any natural resources to satisfy our daily essential needs in one day.

The average U.S. resident , in a year, consumes 275 pounds of meats, uses 635 pounds of paper and uses energy equivalent to 7.8 metric tons of oil. Before, long years ago, the average American ate 197 pounds of meat, used 366 pounds of paper and used energy equivalent to 5.5 metric tons of oil. In the U.S. there is about one passenger car for every two people. Otherwise, Europeans have about one passenger car for every 3.1 people. On the other side, Developing countries have on average, about one passenger car for every 49 people. What does economics have to tell us about these differences in consumption?

Consume sovereignty means the idea that consumer's needs and wants determine the shape of all economic activities. Is this belief valid? That is are the final goals of economic activity all to be found in the act of consumption. Hence, if one day, our earth scarce any kinds of natural resources to be caused shortage, e.g. water, air, oil, land , gas, solar, gas , unclear , wind energy resources as well as foods e.g. vegetables and meats etc. eating resources. Due to human numbers are increasing, such as China, India and Africa etc. developing countries' people numbers are increasing much than the USA, UK etc. developed countries 's people numbers every year. But, our earth's vegetables and pigs, cows, sheet etc. meats foods numbers are decreasing every year. I believe that our foods and vegetables and natural energy resources prices will be influenced to be rose too much due to human demands (wants) are excessive to compare to our earth natural energy resources and meats and vegetables foods supply numbers. On the other side ,if every country's inflation will be increasing , but our salaries will be decreasing, or our salaries will be kept to stable and no changing, even employers will decide to dismiss employees to cause unemployment ratio rising. In result, global consumers' shopping ability will be falling down and crime numbers will be rising by poor, such as developing countries, e.g. Africa, China, India etc. will have many people feel hungry, or who feel diseases , even who will be sick to die from diseases or will be kill to die by crimes. Also , these other factors include foods scarcity, foods and natural energy prices rising, working and home environment pollution etc. factors , these factors can then cause global economic poor , serious inflation ,unbalance incomes reallocation between rich and poor people, discrimination and unfair threat will be caused between countries, even , the war between countries will be caused. Hence, our governments need to concern how to solve our earth natural energy resources and foods and vegetables scarcity challenge , due to which will be caused shortage to supply to human to consume to use or eat in the future on day occurrence. Thus, above reasons can be concluded that as below:

Nowadays, the numbers of human (every country people) are increasing more than just the increasing numbers of consumers' consumption activities , such as our daily essential consumption include meats and vegetables etc. foods and natural energy resources, such as lands, water, gas, oil, wind, water, nuclear, electricity etc. energy . Moreover, natural resources and foods numbers are decreasing due to overpopulation are increasing in developing countries and the numbers of emigration are rising to developing countries, such as UK, USA, France, Germany poor people numbers are increasing due to war or poor issues occur in the developing countries. Moreover, due to the provision consumption activities are most directly address living standard (or lifestyle) goals, which have to do with satisfying basic needs and getting pleasure through the use of natural resources energy provision service demand and vegetables and foods tasty demand by the developed countries' people needs . Also, these poor issues will occur in the developing countries possibly in the future. Due to these factors, I predict our essential consumption , such as foods, vegetables and natural energy resources service provision price will be increasing in global competitive market due to foods and vegetables and energy shortage will be caused by the overpopulation demands rising up and foods and natural energy resources supply numbers falling down factors. Hence, our governments must need to find methods to solve the problem of our essential natural resources shortage and foods scarcity issues occurrence in the future.

Suggestions to solve resources scarcity methods
- Estimation of growth of rural population and income and expected changes of natural resources supply numbers

I recommend developing countries need to estimate growth of rural population and incomes numbers and expected changes numbers in consumption patterns . Taking into account developing countries' known resource capacities and projected development of yields, input use and technologies and making assumptions about their future trading capacity, estimates are also make of future food production level, land use and natural resource numbers import trade demand of developing countries estimation before 2050 year.

Estimation of water natural resources, such as water scarcity agreement on key definitions, the conceptualization of water scarcity in ways that are meaningful for policy development and decision making, the quantification of water scarcity, policy and technical response options available to ensure food security in conditions of water scarcity, criteria and principles that should be used to establish priorities for action to response to water scarcity in agriculture and ensure effective and efficient water scarcity copying strategies. Thus, developing countries will concern to reduce water resources shortage risk. Why is predict water supply important?

During the twentieth century, large multi-purpose dams have served the needs of agriculture, energy and growing cities, and helped protect population from flood hazards. On farm water conservation, particularly the adoption of agricultural practices that reduce runoff to increase the infiltration and storage of water in the soil in rained agriculture is the most relevant local supply enhancement option that farmers have to increase foods production by increasing water availability and decentralized water harvesting conveniently in rural areas for farmers needs. For example, ground water exploitation has grown or in scale. Ground water's capability to provide flexible, on demand water in support of irrigation has been as a major advantage by farmers in rural areas. Thus, farmers need to learn how to reduce water losses increase water productivity and water re-allocation to avoid natural resource of water shortage after 2050 year.

- Renewable natural resources and foods planting sustainability development

The concept of sustainability has become the current answer to absolving our earth of its environment and economic crises in the 21 ST. century. On the one side, the pessimists, usually ecologists and other scientists, who are convinced the earth can't forever support the different countries' demand of renewable and non renewable resources. On the other side, are the optimists, the economists, who are equally convinced that the earth, with market incentives, appropriate public policies, material substitution, recycling and new technology can satisfy the needs and improve the quality of human welfare. Both views are supporting arguments are explored used and sustainable development. Thus, renewable old energy natural resource can keep old energy natural resource to renew to use or research other new energy resource to substitute old natural resource, it will reduce the risk of energy resource shortage if the other new natural resource can be substituted to the old natural energy resource to use in our daily life , such as inventing one kind of new energy resource can be used to substitute gas to drive cars or drive boats or plans or the old gas can be renewed or cycled to use to drive cars or boats or the oil can be renewed or cycled to use to cook. Also, our earth foods, e.g. fruits, vegetables or meats etc. foods if which can be recopied to grow many numbers planting foods from any one kind food or many kinds of foods, such as one meat can be copied to manufacture two to three same kind tasty meats or unlimited same kind tasty meats. I believe the renewable natural resource energy or recopied foods can reduce our foods or energy shortage after 2050 year.

The application of sustainable strategy
between local and national and regional
of international countries

A redefined concept is of the society as whole system, made up of three concentric circles: the economy is found within the society, and both the economy and society exist within the environment. Sustainability indicators are therefore said to attempt to measure the extent to which these boundaries are respected.

I think sustainability measure as a whole concept environment, society and economy. At the bottom of the triangle is the environment or the ultimate means which represents natural resources as a precondition for decent human life. The economy (which includes technology, politics and ethics) is on the next, is not independent but serves as a vehicle for achieving ultimate ends. At the top is equity or society or ultimate end which refers to the wellbeing of the human being.

According to Daly(1990) who indicated "that the economy therefore succeeds to the extent that it conserves and restores ultimate means the environment, and enables the achievement of ultimate ends society equity. This is the application of sustainable strategies to local, national and regional issues, as well as the role of international agencies in local /national strategies." Our earth occurs issues of overpopulation, diseases and political conflict, developed countries also have to deal with problems, such as pollution and unlimited urban expansion with limited resources. Sustainability is the process suggested to improve the quality of human life within the limitations of global environment. It involves solutions for improving human welfare that doesn't result in regarding the environment. We(human) need to concern living within certain limits of the earth's capacity to maintain life, understanding the interconnections among economy, society and environment and maintaining a fair distribution of foods and vegetables and natural energy resources and opportunity for this generation and the next. Thus, on the one side, our governments need to concern three categories: Social/ political, environmental and economic issues are interconnection. Social issues include poverty, consultation, empowerment and culture. Environmental issues include pollution, natural resources and biodiversity/ resilience and economic issues include efficiency, growth and stability. It seems our governments need to considerate social and environment and economic issues to reduce our natural energy resources and foods and vegetables to allocate to let every country people to use fairly.

Reducing global warming and biodiversity
issue occurrence

It seems that we need to know our society will influence our natural environment good or bad. If our society damaged our natural environment, then it will be possible to influence our foods supply of decreasing numbers. e.g. fishes, pigs, cows, sheep and vegetables and fruits etc. foods . Due to bad climate and air and lands and ocean pollution can influence foods can not be grown easily and successfully in farms or fishes can not be lived healthy in ocean. Then, it will cause our meats, fruits and vegetables etc. foods supply shortage. Even, our gas , oil, water etc., natural resources will cause our oceans and lands pollution if human pollute our oceans and lands. In result, our natural resources used numbers will be reduced due to clean lands and oceans are polluted for long time. Finally, natural resources and meats and vegetables and fruits , rice etc. foods prices will be risen due to which are shortage to supply and developing countries' population numbers are increasing which will cause more demand.

Finally, it shall cause many developing countries' poor people who can't eat enough meats, fruits, rice vegetables etc. foods as well as who can't use enough natural resources to attempt to adapt whose past normal daily life, such as lacking enough oil to help them to cook foods to be heat to eat at home or lacked enough water to be boiled to drink. Even, whose health will be poor , then who get diseases to cause die easily when there is no enough oil to buy or enough water to drink. Hence, these developing countries governments need to concern foods and natural resource scarcity problems which will be occurred if who do not find methods to reduce this issue to be occurred after 2050 year.

As Erekson et. al.(1999) concerns about" loss of resources, such as biodiversity or global weather (climate) warming are pacified with the potential of new technology which will lead to greater investments to the future generations for alternative resources and welfare."

Hence, I recommend our governments need to concern global warming or biodiversity issue because of our foods and vegetables and natural resources, such as water, air will be possible polluted to be caused shortage quickly if our earth's global warming or biodiversity issue occurrence to cause our earth's large oceans or lands areas to be polluted. Our governments can attempt to control natural resources , such as oil, gas, water supply into the market and not though the political special conditions to keep them, without considering the political and social standings, which rule the control power and the use of those resources. Such as developed countries can be able to minimize the impact of foods or/and natural resources production and consumption over the natural resources, they are only mechanisms built within an economic rationality, which should be possible to control its people's demand of natural resources, e.g. oil, gas, water and supply of natural resources get more balance. Then these natural resources sale price won't be raised more every year. When there developed countries' people , such as American and Britain who can control to reduce to spend to use the excessive natural resources too much in any time and any place habitually. Then , I believe the developing countries' governments e.g. Africa, China, India, which can buy those developed countries governments' excessive natural resources to raise those developed countries' natural resources supply numbers to provide to whose people to use as well as the most important benefit is that developed countries can gain foreign income from excessive natural resources expectation. Then, these governments will raise GDP economic growth. Hence, if developed countries could control whose people consume natural resource numbers and they could also control to produce natural resource supply numbers . Then, they can gain more excessive natural resources export chance to achieve to raise GDP economic growth aim for long term. As Kirkby et al., (1995)explained "the complexity of sustainable development our natural environment. If our governments can let our earth natural environment gets creation to maintenance, then our natural environment will be reduced the time to degradation. In the long time result, our society rural and urban economy will be growth , then our different countries' global growth will be caused diversity." Hence, it seems different countries' governments need to concern sustainable development to our natural environment .

How to apply agricultural green bio-economy concept to solve control sustainable food consumption and production in a resource-constrained world

Nowadays, challenges for the global food supply have never been so complex. Between now and 2050 year, it has been predicted that growth in the global population and changing diets in developing countries, special in India and China and Africa etc. developing countries which may lead to an increase of around 70% in food demand. At the same time, depletion of fossil hydrocarbons will increase the demand for biomass for biofuels and industrial materials. Hence, developed and developing countries' governments ought need to coordinated to reduce air and water pollution and approached to lands use planning and oceans use planning to supply enough farms to grow potatoes, vegetables, tomatoes, fruits and let cows, pigs, sheep etc. animals can have comfortable and clean farm to live to produce good tasty meats to provide human to eat as well as to reduce pollution to supply fresh and clean water to let fishes to be lived and provides to human to drink clean water. Due to overpopulation will be predicted by scientists after 2050 year, so it will be caused foods and energy shortage possibly. Hence, different countries' governments need have long term perspectives to prepare to have enough foods and energy supply to provide us to eat and use for our earth with resource constraints and environmental limits, and which includes guideline on agricultural research to achieve foods supply aim.

On the one hand, I believe the knowledge-based bio-economy can play in realizing there challenges in particular the balance demand between foods, feed and fuel and the strategic role new technologies can have upon developing a sustainable an green bio-economy. On the other hand, I also think production of the presently high resource dependence and to build more environmentally begin sustainable agriculture system able to feed 9 billion people by

2050 year. I recommend global governments need to concern all aspects of food security including the total food chain and impacts of other land-use and management as well as non food areas, research areas which can be closed to free resources for new priorities, research to manufacture more new unique natural resources, due to gas, oil etc. resources will be used all in one day. On the energy shortage aspect, Substitution of these oil, gas etc. natural resources are needed . For example, nuclear energy is a kind of new natural resource, it can be used to push machines of rockets to be moved in space. In the future, I hope that nuclear energy can be used to drive cars or ships or trains etc. transportation tools in land. Hence, new natural resource research is essential and valid investment to be improved by scientists in the future.

On the global food supply interconnected challenges hand, including climate changes, energy and water supply are further encountered by the financial and economic changes in an increasingly globalized world. As a result, it is unclear how the growing demand for food and bioenergy (both biomass and biofuels) within a wider bio-economy can be met without further compromising ecosystem services on which all economic activities and social depend. I shall emphasizes the interaction of the economic, social and ecological components of our food systems at various levels, with feed backs increasingly the uncertainty and risks relating to future developments.

We need to face the food requirements of a growing world population have to be satisfied and we also need to the face of increasing resource scarcities, such as water, energy and land and foods etc. with the situation further exacerbated by climate change. Thus, we need to focus on our reducing demand through food consumption behavioral changes and structural changes in food systems and food chains change. Due to some developed countries people often to choose to buy these foods to eat excessively e.g. cow meat and pig meat and drink excessive soft drinks, e.g. man-made color juice. So, these developed countries consumers will feel these excessive foods and soft drinks can be rubbish if these developed countries consumers often drink these man-made color juice and eat pig and cow meats often excessively. It seems who ought to change their diet behavior and food consumption to avoid to spend too much money to buy excessive foods and drinks and who often shall not decide to eat and drink them when who feel not hungry habitually . Hence, changing human diet habit is one important psychology factor to reduce water and foods shortage, due to the meats and juices can be reduced to be rubbish if human can learn how to control their diet habit to reduce to consume excessive meats and vegetables and rice and soft drinks etc. kind of foods and drinks. Then, I believe that food and water drinking numbers will be reduced too much in the future. Hence, different countries' governments need to educate whose people to know that why who will face foods and water scarcity possibly and to let who to know how the issue can be avoided to cause by the changing of their diet habit and consumption behavior. Teaching includes, such as let who to learn why resources scarcities are expected to reduce and defining food security concept, the need is for a better understanding of complexity of vegetable systems, the need to improve the diversity and response capacity of food systems to enhance resilience, the need to address both food consumption and production, knowledge generation and innovation through cross-sector approaches is essential and the need for agricultural knowledge and innovation systems that are fit for farming purpose. After developed countries' people are educated to let who to know why who need to reduce to consume excessive foods and soft drinks habitually to aim to avoid the chance of foods and water supply shortage will be occurred after 2050 year.

On the other side, in the case of biodiversity, the loss of functional biodiversity destabilizes ecosystems and weakens their ability to deal with natural disasters or human induced stresses, such as pollution and climate change. Hence, scientists need to research how to reduce new diseases to cause foods and water pollution, even new diseases cause to influence human health. Due to unpredictable new diseases will be caused foods, fruits, vegetables etc. can't be grow easily , even cows, pigs, sheep etc. animals are not health to cause diseases to be died easily. Then, those new diseases will be decreases our foods supply numbers seriously.

Resources scarcities are expected to define future food security. The predominant form of agriculture, food processing and retailing relies heavily on cheap inputs and the potential impact on this of long term resource scarcity trends has been largely overlooked. Scarcities are either biophysical limits, such as resource supply and availability or environment limits relating to pollution and its impacts on ecosystems and the global climate system. Hence, every country's government ought to educate to let whose citizen to discuss how to protect future food security topic to avoid resource scarcities occurrence after 2050 year. We need to know we are facing pollution (e.g. land, water, energy) and related to environmental limits e.g. climate change, ocean acidification and biodiversity loss. They represent a real threat, not only to future food supplies, but also to global stability and prosperity, through increasing poverty to developing countries and impacts on international trade, finance and investments.

Hence, pollution and environmental limits will have direct relationship to influence every countries' foods supply numbers , then it will influence every country's gross domestic product income if the consumption is reduced by foods inflation. For example, the combined effect of climate change and bio-diversity which makes the food production systems poorly due to a reduced resilience to shocks and changes over the long term , such as the limited availability of ore resources, soil degradation to loss of biodiversity. Both of these require a long term strategic approach to research and an openness to new research directions. These will need to help provide solutions towards more sustainable food consumption and production, some of which will need to break with current farmers or food manufacturers way of producing food methods. For example, research into ecological approaches: foods nutrient and water clean management and replacement of energy intensive inputs are priorities. Research to support energy efficient technologies for use in the food chain is also needed. Industry should assist in tackling the forthcoming challenges with new business models that can support the decoupling of resource use and changing consumption excessive foods behaviors and improving health foods production methods. For instance, changing the foods supply chains) e.g. more local purchasing) may have huge impacts on costs and also on creating closer links and confidence between producers and consumers.

In conclusion, different countries need find methods to solve foods and energy scarcity problem before 2050 year. I recommend that who can attempt to solve earth warm climate, innovate agricultural production and supply system, change human diet habit and food consumption of behavior, co-operate the trade of foods and energy demand and supply between countries fairly and reasonably, reduce food and natural resource waste, renew and recopy new kind of foods, research new natural resource substitution etc. different methods. However, if every country government can attempt to find any one or more of these methods to solve food scarcity to avoid to occur before 2050 year. I believe that the food scarcity challenge won't be occur after 2050 year in the future.

CHAPTER VIII

Electronic vehicle how influences future gas vehicle market changes

Nowadays, since electronic vehicle invention, it brought competition to fight traditional gas vehicle martet. Electronic vehicle is only needed to be charged battery, then battery will bring energy to push the electornic car to be driven fastly. So traditional vehicle market is experiencing decline life cycle stage. When, electronic vehicle is popular to be accepted to every drivers. In fact, when we drive cars on the roads, our cars will have gas emission to polluate our sir. Earth warmth is dramatically increasing. The main reason is that global air is polluted, e.g. frequent driving activities will bring air pollution when gas emission is caused. Hecnce, environment vehicle is only needed to charged battery. Every time battery charged can bring one day driving time power or enerty to let drivers to drive . So, basing on environmental protection and battery long time driving both reasons, it brings strengths to electronic vehicle to persuade global any drivers to choose to buy electronic vehicle more than traditional gas vehicle.

I shall research these questions: These questions may concern: Will the gas vehicle be influenced to experience the decline life cycle stage rapidly when the electronic vehicle is accepted to be popular to drive ? Can traditional gas vehicle avoid decline life cycle stage comes as well as if traditional gas vehicle real prepares to experience decline life cycle stage ? Can it re-grow to change to enter growth life cycle stage again? Can new electronic vehicle market influence traditional gas vehicle market to shorten time to experience decline life cycle age rapidly?

In our driving history, cars invention had helped us do not need to spend long walking time to go to anywhere conveniently. In fact, due to technological limit, e.g. bus, taxi, tram, train must use gas to be energy to push them to be driven on the roads. When car invention period, or it may call car market birth life cycle stage period. In the 1800 year beginning , human does not know what car function or why we need car. When cars had been invented, it is global whole car industry borth life cycle stage period. This period its characteristics are: In societies , people accepted car tools to drive on the roads. Many people feel to spend money to buy cars, it is waste money, because they may choose to catch any kinds of public transport tools, e.g. bus, train, tram, taxi, ferry, undergroundtrain to arrive any destinations conveniently. So, from 1800 year to 1900 year, global whole car industy had been still keeping in the growth life cycle stage. Because in global society, many people hasd been general accepting public tranposrt tools, their fee are vey cheap and passengers can spend short time to catch them to go to anywhere, they can provide long transport service time for office working people, student from morning to evening time. Hence, this 100 years period, global car sale number could not significant increase, because public transport tools could bring convenience to any one when they needed to leave homes to arrive far away destination in short time.

Hence, global car industry ought not develop rapidly, because many peoplecould not accept to spend money to buy cars to replace to catch any public transport tools. But after 1900 year, global whole gas vehicle industry began to experience growth life cycle stage. Because global many people had jobs to do, unemployment ratio begain to reduce. In society, rich people number began to increase. It based on theseboth factors: families began to consider to attempt to buy any kinds of cars in order to attempt to buy any kinds of cars in order to let them to feel enjoyable to drive to go to anywhere. So, from 1901 year to 2000 year, it may be global whole gas vehicle market growth life cycle stage . In this period, global car buyers number had been increasing significantly . In average, global every family may own at least one car, even more. It depends on whether how many members number, the family has and whether the family has how many member(s), he/she has own one car licence. Moreover, in society, many people began to accept second hand cars, because second hand cars must be chaper to compare new cars as well as it is real one good choice for the low income car buyer social consumer groups in society. So, in this global vehicle market growth life cycle stage, instead of new car buyers number had been increasing significantly, the second hand car buyers number had also been increasing significantly in the same time. So, global new cars and secod hand car buyers number had increased rapidly every year, because global population is increasing. It also caused many working people did not like to spend long time to queue to wait public transport tools, it is another factor to persuade people chooce to buy cars to drive to go to offices or schools or anywhere in their relax time, e.g. holiday, sunday. So, this 100 year, may be global whole car industry growth life car cycle stage.

After 2000, it may be global car industy mature life cycle ctage , many car manufacturers begun to innovate any kinds of traditional cars to change to advanced engine function, auto-window, auto dooe functions , navigation road locaion search function, even non-manual driven artificial intelligent car invention. So, after 2000 year, due to global car buyers begun to pursue comfortable drivin feeling. They need to pursue comfortable driving feeling. They need to buy unique design of cars, or more functions of cars to drive on the road . Hence, global different unique function and styles of cars purchase needs had been significant increasing. Moreover, car prices had also been increasing more, due to more different unique functional and styles of car purchase needs had been increasing in order to satisfy the rich or high income car buyers group. So, after 2000, it may be global car market 's mature life cycle stage.

But, I believe that global car market's mature life cycle stage can not keep long time. The main reason is because the electronic car invention. After 2000 year, since one kind of new transport tool of electronic car invention, it influences many gas car owners or non car owners feel interesting to learn how to drive electronic cars and feel whether what advantages that electronic cars can satisfy their driving needs. IN special, environmental protection awareness drivers must believe electornic cars can reduce air pollution when they choose to drive them on the roads , due to none gas emission effect to pollute our earth air. When they choose to drive electronic cars, due to they only need to charge battery, then their electronic cars can be driven on the roads in short time rapidly. Even, report also indicated driving electronic cars accident occurrence chance may be also influenced to reduce to compare driving gas cars usually. So, electronic vehicle market may be future main competitor to global traditional gas vehicle market. May electronic vehicle invention influence future gas vehicle shorten time to experience to decline life cycle stage rapidly? How gas vehicle market may avoid the shorten time to experience decline life cycle stage if electronic vehicle market may influence its development in global car manufacture industry? I shall attempt to solve these challenges as below:

IN fact, electronic vehicle innovation is not long time , so the global electronic vehicle manufacturing and sale market is experiencing birth life cycle stage. Can electronic vehicle market reduce to shorten time to experience growth, even mature life cycle stages. It depends on these factors:

The factors may affect battery electronic vehicle energy consumption and driving behavior impact. They may include whether environment protection awareness will increase or decrease to global nay one gas car owners or non car owners. Because if global environment protection awareness increase, it will influence gas car owners or non car owners (potential either battery electronic vehicle energy or gas vehicle energy car choice buyers), begun to feel their frequent driving gas vehicle behaviors may bring air pollution or global warming, temperature rises weather disaster occurrence in the future. They alsoknow battery electronic vehicle energy consumption price may be cheap to same to gas vehicle energy consumption. Moreover, they may feel that if they change to drive battery electronic vehicles, it may help them to minimize environmental air pollution impacts of the end of life stage and brings positive impacts on improving climate change and air quality for our future. So, if many car owners or non car owners feel that they have responsibility to protect our climate environment pollution. Then, battery electronic vehicle buyers number will have possible to increase rapidly in short time. Due to the significant impact of gas vehicle and battery electronic vehicle their life cycle analysis can be utilized to analyze the advantages and disadvantages to cause car buyers make comparison between them and gas vehcile and battery electronic vehcile both kinds vehicles are highly complex supply chain choice in the automobile industry nowadays. Moreover, due to carbon intensity of this stage was calculated from emission factors at the global car manufacture industry. Hence, emission factor may be one important influential factor to influence any one makes car purchase decision or either gas or battery electronic car purchase decison.

For example , in our societies, if many peopl own environment protection awareness, then global gas vehicle buyers number may be influenced to reduce, even the owning gas vehicle families may be influenced to choose to buy battery electronic cars to replace their gas cars. They may sell their gas vehicles to any one, even to steel manufacturers easily. Hence, gas vehicle on steel existence number may also reduce ot they can disappear in our road in short time rapidly. If batttery electronic vehcile can be popular to accept to drive on the road to any one driver in our societies. Then, battery electronic cars may be influenced to increase driving needs to any one driver. it's sale number may also influenced to increase rapidly. Consequently, it may have chance to experience to growth life cycle stage from birth life cycle stage in short time rapidly in global whole electronic car manufacturer and sale market.

Then another influential factor concerns how owning car consumers feel the charge of the battery energy use of resources in comparison to conventional gas energy use of resources to driving cars. In combination with the regional electricity mix these factors influence the energy materials for a specific car market. For these first life cycle phases a range of values is possible to battery electronic car market. If in our societies, there are many people choose to use battery charge energy resource to drive electronic cars, their prices are very reasonable to compare gas vehicles or they feel gas will face rapid shortage challenge, if global any one only likes to drive gas vehicle. Then, they may be influenced to choose to buy the battery electronic vehicles to replace gas vehicles. Hence, enery resource used to car my also be one main factor to influence any one car buyer individual either battery electronic car or gas vehicle purchase choice.

Hence, it implies that the life style environmental impacts and energy resource used both impacts of battery electronic cars are a topic of increasing relative importance of the vehicle production stage and the maximum impact on climate change (ingc02/km) that is observed by many climate scientists, their observation to climate change good or bad change effect may influence global battery electronic vehicle needs. So, how clean are battery electric cars, it will be one popular topic for environmental scientists to environmental protection awareness car owners and non car owners. T o analysis hoe to cause electric car life cycle changes. The arrival of the electric car has brought with it an array of life cycle factors that influence the carbon emission level to any one country's environment.

Influence of national electricity grid over the use phase, so it implies that if the country feels carbon emission level is high , due to gas vehicle may bring carbon emission to pollute air to the country. Although, factory's carbon emission or airplane carbon emisson may be one factor to influence the country's air pollution level to be increase. The year has high carbon emission level, it considers gas vehicle air carbon emission level whether it is high or low in the year. So, if the country's gas vehicle car owners number is sudden increasing rapidly. Consequently, it will evaluate that the car increasing number may influence the country itself carbon emission level to be high and it may cause air pollution seriously.

Hence, battery electric car industry life cycle whether when it can experience growth life cycle stage or mature life cycle stage from birth life cycle stage, it depends on what carbon emisson level to any one country. If this year has many countries believe their high carbon emissin level is due to gas vehicle 's carbon emission causes. Then, this high carbon emission level report factor may raise many car owners or non car owners consider environment protection awareness and it may also influence many car buyers choose to buy battery electric cars to replace gas cars to drive on the road frequently in this year.

Also in order to avoid themselves countries' air pollution is more serious. Hence, global carbon emission rise or fall level and any one environmental protection awareness psychological both factors may influence future battery electric car market development. They may have close relationship to influence any one traditional gas vehicle owner to buy one new battery vehicle vehicle to replace it to drive on the road, or any one potential car purchaser makes final battery electric car or gas vehicle decision absolutely.

On conclusion, above these factors may explain whether it is possible that battery electronic vehicle invention may influence future gas vehicle market changes to decline life cysle stage from mature life cycle stage. It depends on whether environmental protection awareness to car owners increasing or decreasing number , carbon emission level whether it is high or low, gas energy resource facing shortage factors to influence future electronic vehicle need.

Chapter 9

Factors influence public transport service industry reaches

life cycle decline stage

In our future road public transport service development. Does underground train improvement bring another new public transport service experience to let passengers to experiece another new road public transport service replace traditional bus, tram, train, taxi , rapid speed train etc. public transport tool service by this kind new " exceed sound speed" underground train public transport tool? Can this kind of " exceed sound speed" underground train public service transport tool replace traditional bus, train, tram, taxi, road piblic transport tools ? Will traditional road public transport tools experience to reach decline life cycle service stage from maturity life cycle service stage in soon future possible, if this kind of " new exceed sound speed innovation underground train is invented ?

What is exceed sound speed underground train ? It can run exceed sound speed to catch above four to eight passengers to sit in the small size circle shape underground train from one distination to another destination in short time. For example, it can run at exceed sound speed at underground from US Washington city to New York city, in the future, it will be possible one kind of small circle size underground train, it may only catch about one to eight passengers every journey, when this kind of new exceed sound speed underground train was really invented. Can it replace traditional slow speed underground train and road public transport tools to be accepted by many passengers? In this US future new exceed sound speed small size underground train public transport tool case, it only needs spend half hour to transport passengers from US Washington to New York city rapidly. In general, underground train speed needs about three hours from Washington to New York city distance. So, it can shorten time to let passengers to avoid any delay. The question is that : Can it influences future global public transport service life cycle stage to reach decline life service cycle life in short time, if this kind of new exceed sound speed small size underground train public transport tool is invented in success? I shall attempt to answer whether future new sound speed rapid small size underground public tranport service train invention, it will influence other traditional public transport tools to reach the decline life service cycle stage rapidly in short time as below:

In our traditional public transport development history, since 1900, human had been beginning to consider every country ought own themselves public transport fools, e.g. for passengers service. So, passengers can pay cheap ticket to catch either bus, or tram, or train ot ferry, or taxi, or underground train from one destination to another destination in short time conveniently. So, public transport tool needs had been popular increasing, because there were not many people like to buy cars to drive when any kinds of public tranport tools are invented in 1900 beginning. The reason may be that they feel expensive gas expenditure and cars will need to repair or become old etc. different reasons. So, from 1900, public transport tool service tools may be whole public transport service industry's birth life cycle service stage. In this stage, global any passengers had been attempting to choose to catch either bus, trains, trams, taxi, underground trains etc. public transport tools to go to anywhere conveniently. They would compare whether public transport service can provide comfortable feeling and rapid transport service quality to be better than purchase one car to drive.

Hence, in this global public transport service birth life cycle stage, global human had been attempting any kinds of public transport tools catching feeling whether which one kind could bring more comfortable service feeling , e.g. bus service is better or tram service is better or train service is better or underground train service is bettr or ferry service is better. Hence, in global whole public transport industry tools will be compared by all passengers . Passengers will choose the best kind of public transport tool to catch in any time when they feel need. Hence, bus, taxi, train, tram, underground train, ferry transport service performance level must bee very high to avoid their passengers to make decision to choose another kind of public transport service to replace them.

From 1900 to 1950, global public transport service had been experiencing fair or birth stage competition because any one passenger had been attempting to choose which kind of public transport tool to replace purchase car need. After 1950, global public transport service had been experiencing growth life cycle service stage. Because many people began to feel different kinds of public transport tools prices are cheap and reasonable . So global had had many different transport tools to replace purchase cars needs to anyone. Also, bus, taxi, ferry, train, tram , underground train number and transport service frequent time will need to increase in order to satisfy increasing passengers transport service needs in transport service market.

After 1990, global transport service industry had been experiencing mature life cycle service stage, instead of non owning car people must need to catch any kinds of public transport tools to go to aywhere, even owning car people, when they feel that they often drive cars, frequent driving car behavior may bring high gas expenditure in long time. So, when they feel any one kind of transport tool can transport them to go to anywhere conveniently in short time. On the day, they will not drive themselves cars to go to anywhere, they will choose any one kind of public transport tools to go to the destination on that day, because they do not want to spend much gas expenditure or avoid traffic jam or accident occurrence when they need to go to the destination in shor time.

So, in this mature public transport service life cycle stage, global any one includes owning car person and non owning car person, we had been accepted to choose any one kind of public transport tool to replace cars to go to any destinations conveniently. Because bus stations number increased, bus number increases, bus can arrive in short time, taxi, train, tram , ferry , underground train public transport tools services can follow bus service to provide accurate shorten arrival time, comfortable catching environment, reasonable price, none delay arrival time, high passengers transport service quality to let global any one passenger to feel satisfactory. Hence, after 1980, global public transport service had been experiencing mature life cycle service stage.

Global public tranport service needs had been increasing. At the same time, when any one kind of public transport tool is popular to be accepted to choose to catch by any one passenger. In this suitation, if one kind of public transport tool is improved, e.g. shorten transport distance, arrival destination time can be decreased, price is reasonable cheap, such as Japan rapid speed train, China, prior rapid speed train etc. These rapid speed electric trains can transport many passengers from one station to another station in short time. So, in road train service industry, nowadays, it is experiencing mature life cycle service stage. It means that any passengers will be influenced to catch this kind of rapid speed train in prefer to compare tram, traditional old speed train, bus, ferry to catch.

However, in the future, it is possible that one kind of underground train may be invented successfully. It is short circle size underground train, it can catch one to maximum eight passengers only for every journey in underground. Nowadays, US scientists had been attempting to manufacture this kind of " exceed sound speed'" underground train, if it can be invented in success, it may catch maxium eight passengers from Washington to New York city within half hour time . In general, traditional US underground train needs two to three hours to catch passengers from Washington underground train station to New York underground train station. So, if this kind of " exceed sound speed" underground train is invented in success, it will be possible to influence global public transport train, tram, bus, ferry, taxi, public transport tool passengers number may be influenced to reduce, due to its fee is reasonable cheap, more comfortable, rapid destination arrival and on time arrival transport service etc. factors.

The question is that: How this kind of " exceed sound speed underground train tool" bring positive or negative changes to influence global public transport service life cycle stage?

Nowadays, rapid speed train or underground train public service transport tool had changed traditional gas energ train or electric train transport service need to mature life cycle stage. Since electric train or rapid speed train invention. This kind of public transport had provided one kind of more comfortable and rapid transport service choice to any passengers. So, train or underground train transport tool compares to general bus, tram , ferry to experience rapid mature life service cycle stage. Many passengers many feel to catch underground train or train in preference because their ticket prices are reasonable cheap and they are provided rapid short time journey to arrive any destinations any any countries. For London underground is a rapid transit system serving greater histry . These two ran electric trains in circular tunnels having diameters.

In 1933, most of London's underground railways, tramway and bus services are accepted in popular . Hence, UK, LOndon railway public transport tool has developed long time. The average speed on the London underground is 20.5 miles per hour, including station stops. On Metropolitan line, trains can reach over 60 mph. The shortest distance between teo adjacent stations on the network is only 260 metres and the longest is 6.3 kilometres.

Nowadays, the fastest underground train is the Victoria line, it can reach speeds up tp 50 mph because the stations are further apart. The metropolitan line has the fastest train speeds, sometimes reaching over 60 mph. IS light rail faster than buses? IN fact the data is from the National trainsit database website and it shows that it costs almost twice as much, one average to move one light rail vehicle per hour versus onw bus. Hence, light rail must be faster than buses, comparing rail versus bus trainsit transport service life cycle stages, rail versus may reach mature transport service life cycle stage. Otherwise, bus transit transport service life cycle stage will be possible to be influenced to experience decline life service cycle stage from nowadays mature stage. The reason is that future " sound speed underground rail transport will be possibe to invent successfully. Then, this kind improved exceed sound speed underground train transport tool may replace to traditional electric train or underground electric rail, when any countries passengers can accept to choose to catch this kind of developed " exceed sound speed" underground rail tranport tool in habit. In fact, underground rail versus bus tranit focus primary on vehicle travel speeds and operating, per capita vehicle travel grew rapidly between 1970 and 2000. If one day, US " exceed sound speed" underground short size rail is invented successfully., it will change the whole traditional public tranport service industry mode to persuade passengers to enjoy this kind " exceed sound speed feeling" and choose to catch this kind public transport service in preference, due to they can enjoy rapid short time destination arrival journey, and it can bring benefit to transport providers for lifecycle saving energy and emission carbon pollutants reduces. It may reach the rail public transport tool invention to the topest mature life cycle service stage, if this kind of exceed sond speed underground train can be invented successfully. It means that rail transport service industry only needs to spend less developing time to reach the mature life cycle service stage from birth and growth life cycle service stages .

In global whole public transport service life cycle development stage, underground rail transport tool is the most rapid experiencing the topest mature life cycle service stage of only one kind public transport tool to compare bus, ferry, tram , train . Although, transport infrastructure has long operational life, there are too many urban public transport networks, including light rail (metro and tram), but if the kind of new " exceed sound speed" underground rail can be real invented. Then, in underground rail public transport tool development history, it will help underground electric rail development to let any passengers to feel more comfortable, most rapid, reasonable ticket price and convenient underground journeys in every day.

Hence, if it can be invented successfully, it will not only help whole rail transport service to reach mature life service cycle stage or it will be future the best or the most comfortable one kind of using public transport tool choice to global any passengers by 2041. Because when it could real be invented in success, it proved that it may fight physical barriers and fast moving or elevated sound speed levels can cause that any passengers can feel more comfortable and none long time distance to arrive destination anywhere. For example, if this kind of exceed sound speed underground short size rail transport tool can transport US passengers from tunnel to go through ocean to another countries stations. Then, any one does not need to catch airplane transport or ship to go to another country easily. They can catch it to go through ocean underground tunnels to any country from ocean in short time also. So, instead of this kind of sound speed underground rail can replace traditional tram, train, transport service on the road, even it can also replace airplanes and ships, ocean and air transport service by 2041 in the future. So, its transport inventio may change global traditional transport mode, it can provide underground ocean tunnel and underground and tunnel transport channels to arrive any underground road tunnel transport channels to arrive any destinations conveniently. Then, it can bring shop and airplane transport service changes to let wholc passengers to have more one kind of new transport tool choice, such as underground exceed sound speed rail feeling need. So, ship and airplane transport service life cycle may also be influenced to experience decline life cycle service cycle stage after 2041, if this kind of exceed sound speed short circle size underground rail could be invented in success to catch any countries passengers spend short time to catch it to go to another countries' underground rail stations from himself/herself country's underground rail station by ocean tunnel conveniently.

Consequently, future exceed sound speed underground short circle size rail public transport tool invention may influence other kinds of public transport tools to experience and reach decline life cycle service stage early after 2041, if it can real invent successfully by 204. Hence, it explains that why bus, tram, train, ferry, airplane transport tools need to continue to invent or improve rapid flying speed or rapid flight speed and comfortable feeling quality in order to fight this kind of future new exceed sound speed underground rail transport tool to avoid rapid decline life cycle service stage easily after 2041. So, " this kind of exceed sound speed small circle size underground rail" transport tool invention " it will bring global other different kinds of road and sea and air transport tool will face decline life service cycle stage early after 2041 in possible.

Why social behavior may influence organizational strategy needs to be changed

Any organizations may experience organizational life cycle stages from birth stage to growth stage to maturity , then it may also experience decline and/or regrow stages. But this two stages, they are not all organizations must may attempt to experience. It depends on whether economic environment how changes, organizational itself SWOT strengths and weaknesses etc. unpredicted factors to influence that when the organization will experience decline life cycle stage. It means that if the organization has very poor performance, then the organization has possible to experience decline life cycle stage in short time or long time. Otherwise, if the organizationhas very good performance, it ought not experience decline life cycle stage in short time, when it can reach mature stage in its the topest level. Even, when the organization has poor performance, so it is experiencing decline stage, but if it may implement effective strategies to help itself organization to develop . Then, if its strategies are very effective , in consequence, the organization ought may experience regrowing stage to re-experience its mature life cycle stage again. So, it seems that if the organization can have very good performance. Client number can increase significant as well as profit can also growth rapidly. Then, the organization ought may experience long time in mature life cycle stage or it means that it will be difficult to reach decline life cycle stage. Unless, some sudden inpredicted economic environment, or strong competitors etc. influence its performance, then they will have chance to cause it experiences to decline life cycle stage from mature stage suddenly. Hence, all organizations must need to experience birht life cycle stage in beginning to this stage.

However, when the business founder starts to set up his/her business. He/she needs time to deal any difficulties,e.g. how to advertise his/her products to let customers have much knowledge, promote them to sell to market, how to implement strategies to solve organizational challenges. So, in birth stage, any organizations ought feel difficult to improve its whole performance or evaluate whether its future performance can improve to be better or can not improve or worse. Then, when the organization operates one period, it ought experience to growth stage, but it still depends on external factors to influence whether when it may experience growth stage, the factors may include: Whether strategies can be effective, economic environment is good or bad, customers purchase desire level is high or loe, cost expenditure is high or low etc. difficult factor.

So, before any organizatons may experience growth stage, there are many different complex factors to influence whether they can succeed to experience this stage easily. If the organization can not implement any effective strategies to solve its customers purchase emotion challenges, then its business is difficult to continue grow, also it means that the organization can not growor expand its business easily. Due to it can not continue to develop its business easily. It must not reach mature life cycle stage easily. Thus, any organizations can reach mature life cycle stage. It represents that its business has good strategies to solve any challenges in order to its products can attract customers to choose to buy or it can provide good service performance to satisfy clients needs to compare irs competitors in this market successfully.

In fact, it is not all organizations can attempt to experience the mature life cycle stage. This stage is any organization individual the topest stage. In this stage, the organization may have many clients increasing number significantly every year, its market can continue expand, profit can continue increases . All is the best to any organizations, if it can reaches this stage . All many organizations may only experience birth stage or growing stage . They reach this either birth or growth stage, then they have none good strategies to compete their clients number can not increase, but only decreases, profit reduces , even loss. They can not know how to change strategied to improve their performance or competitive effort to fight this competitors. Then, their businesses can not continue grow or expand. So, they have more chance to experience decline stage after either birth or growth stage only. They can not reach mature life cycle stage to attempt the topest level in whole business (organizational) life cycle stage or process. Thus, it brings these questions: Why do organizations need to learn organizational life cycle stages? What advantages to bring if they can attempt to learn how to reach growth or mature life cycle stages easily? I shall explain as below:

● Why do organizations need to spend time to learn how may experience different business life cycle stages?

The business life cycle is the progression of a business in phases over time and is most commonly divided into five stages: Launch or birth, growth, maturity and decline or regrow. Each company begins its operations as a business and usually by launching new products or services. Because any organizations will encounter challenges in every stages . If they know what factos may help them to enter another new stage of business life cycle or what challenges may threaten them can not enter another new business life cycle stage easily. Because businessman need to learn and how adjust their business model to ensure profitability. That is why an awareness of what stage of the business life cycle , you are currently it can be helpful. Hence, how to maximize each stage of the business life cycle, the businessmen might still need to learn how to work in order to improve performance when the businessmen are experiencing any one life cycle stage. Moreover, each business life cycle stage comes still need to learn how to turn a profit and the first outlines of their governance and compliance and this is one big reason why most businesses fail at this stage.

So, I assume that business life cycle stage is similar to school examination, the student needs to spend time to learn in the birth learning stage, then he needs to test in the growth learning stage, next is examination in the mature learning stage, if the student fails, t is decline learning stage to the school. It may be due to the teachers can not teach students to learn easily. So, these are many students fail in tests or examinations. So, if the school teachers can improve teaching methods to let many students may earn high grades in tests or examinations. Then, the school may experience growth, even mature teaching life cycle stage in short time rapidly . Hence, teaching quality can improve or not , it will influence any school organizations ought feel to schools to learn how to improve teaching methods or strategies in order to let students can experience the maturity learning stage or it can also experience the maturity teaching stage. It means that it ought learn how to improve its teachers teaching service performance to satisfy students learning needs if it hopes to reach maturity learning and teaching life cycle stage in short time for itself school organization benefit.For example, the organization founder may ask himself/herself why he/she wants to start this business, learns how to manage exployees strategies? It is the learning needs in the third stage, such as maturity stage. Otherwise, in the first stage of the business entity birth life cycle is sometimes called the seed stage and a matter of iteraing, testing an learning , and trying again, knowing that the businessman is unlikely to have.

What advantages may bring to the organization if it can attempt to learn how to solve different challenges in different business life cycle stages ? What advantages to the organization, if it can know how to experience every business life cycle stage?

In fact, the business life cycle is the progression of a business in phases over time, and is consumer segments by advertising their comparative advantages and vale. For example, when the business is experiencing growth stage , in the growth phase, the business founder needs to spend time to learn how his company can experience rapid sales growth. This learning may assist his business to develop his business to enter next mature how stage easily , for example, he can learn how the rapid growth stage takes advantage from the proven sales model, e.g. online sale or traditional visiting shop sale model which is more suitable to his business, marketing model and operations model, e.g. how to advertise his product or promote his products can affect more audiences concern this will see the businessmen's jounrey from idea to start up, and if successful, how to keep to stay long time in the mature stage. Rememeber, when having a successful business model behind any businessmen is undoubtedly an advantage, it is not a disadvantage when the founder spends more time to learn hoe to run his business. In fact, he won't waste his time to learn how to improve his business in different business life cycle stages. So, a tactical plan will take any business strengths and reduces to avoid weakness cause to influence its development. So, knowing where you small product is in its product life cycle, it is important to continue to develop your business successfully. SO, any impacts of all life cycle stages, any businesses need to be considered comprehensively , for one new technological product firm example, its new technological product life cycle begins with the introduction or birth stage. The high technological product company must succeed at both developing new product and managing them in the face of changing tastes, competitors' technologies similar change. So, it is what it needs to learn in this stage for this new product technological firm preparing development to next growth stage.

On the conclusion, learning how to achieve in every business life cycle stage, it can bring these benefits to any organizations, such as : they can understand and redefine this role from a more, if the organization ony to learn sale frameworks what it could have picked up. It is not enough, because most organizations will only find that a majority of their total sale number which is to use solely supplier-specific data about the life cycle, but they neglect how to set targets to learn how to improve their sale to be better in the future time, it is one important factor explain why many organizations only reach the growth stage, but they can not experience to next mature stage more easily, due to they do not consider how to implement strategies in order to achieve their next targets. They feel often implment targets which will help them to know whether they need to how to do in order to improve their businesses to satisfy clients needs. As with any effort in your organization, communication plays a critical role, craft machine learning to predict and manage human for remote teams to work through the innovation lifecycle, serve them well. Any organizations need to learn how to satisfy any customer individual purchase jounrey (called purchase experience) which the customer has with the organization, because when the organization can learn how to satisfy any client individual real need in any life cycle stage. On consequence, its clients number with have possible to influence increase. Thus, any organizations can bot neglect to learn how to satisfy client individual real purchase experience need in any life cycle stages because improvement to salepeople sale performance, they need spend time to learn in every time sale experience . When the organization can build excellent sale teams, then they may help it to build famous loyalty and good client relationship in order to expand its business more easily. Hence, in any businesses' life cycle stages, they must need to spend time to learn how to improve product quality service performance to bring customers' satisfactory emotion in order to expand their business developmenr more easily. So, i recommend that all small organizations expand to large size, they must need time to learn and attempt to find the best methods to solve any difficulties when they are facing in any one business cycle stage, if they want to expand their businesses successfully.

● The relationship between learning change management and rapid
reaching mature life cycle

It is one good question: Can the manager or CEO help whole organization to develop rapidly if he/she attempt to learn how to help his/her organization to implement different strategies to solve different challenges in different business life cycle stages? Does it easy to help the organization to grow up when a learning CEO or learning manager accepts to learn anything to compare a non learning manager in different business life cycle stages? Has it relationship between learning or non learning manager and rapid experiencing business life cycle stage and rapid developing business growth? I shall attempt to explain as below:

In fact, it is not essential to any managers or CEOs need to spend time to learn how any why what factors may influence their organizations to grow up to next business life cycle stage, but in comparison one learning how to change organizational life cycle stages manager and non-learning how to change organizational life cycle stages manger. Can learn attitude or strategy to help the manager to develop or expand his organization to next life cycle stage more easily or rapidly? I shall attempt to explain as below:

In fact, any organizations expect to change to next life cycle stage in success , can the manager(s) learn how to implement strategies to achieve to change management to their organizations' development in success? How the organizational management learns how to adapt organizational management change, it may be one important factor to influence whether the organization needs to spend how long time to reach growth life cycle stage from birth stage or reach mature life cycle stage from growth stage. So, it seems that how management spends time to learn how to change his/her organization. It will have relationship to the organization needs to spend long time to reach next life cycle stage successfully.

Hence, learning how to train employees in each life cycle stage, it is the important factor to influence any organizations succeed, the employee lifecycle is an ongoing process that starts and ends with competent employees in any managers' organizations. There are nine elements ofa successful change management process, if the organizational management expects whole organization can real reach to next life cycle stage in success. The nine elements of a successful change management process, any management needs to spend time to learn. They may include: readiness assessments, communication planning implementation, sponsor activities and sponsor roadmaps organizing, organizatons need to provide change management training for managers to learn how to achieve effectiveness as well as providing training development and delivery learning methods to them, resistance management learning and learning employee feedback and corrective action. Moreover, managements also need to spend time to learn change management steps in order solve any challenges in order to reach next life cycle stage easily.

The change management learning steps may include: Step 1: Urgency creation , step 2: Building every team serves to every department efficiently, learning how to create avision, how to communication of division, how to remove obstacles, going for quick wins, let the change mature, integrate the change. These elements are incorporated into change management phases process. For example, some elements of communication planning occur early in the lifecyle. At this stage, change management is not fully achieved effectively, so management needs to spend more time to learn how to achieve effective communication planning in order to achieve effective communication planning in order to keep whose organization employees can communicate to work efficiently. Also, it will help client service employees to know how to build good communication management method to deal or answer or satisfy their clients' sale service and improving service performance absolutely.

Because organizations are nor statis, they change , if one organization still stays long time in birth stage, it represents that the organization feels difficulties to continue develop . So, the management needs to find whether what challenges threaten its organization can not reach growth stage more easily. One failure changing management organization, it has these characteristics: failure to change, inexperienced management, not enough revenue, inadequate leadership. Hence, it has close relationship between employee life cycle and organizational life cycle . If the organizational management expects its organization can continue develop or reaches next life cycle stage in success, it needs to learn how to let employees to adapt when its organization is changing in order to keep efficience and improving service performance absolutely . So, I believe that it has relationship between learning change management and reaching to mature business cycle stage rapid and achieving long time staying in business cycle mature stage .

The question concerns that how management can learn to implement change management strategy in order to let his organization can reach mature cycle stage in short time as well as keep to stay in this mature life cycle stage in long time?

Firstly, we need to know what change management life cycle means ? For information technological industry example, it may be explained that the change management process is designed to help control of the life cycle of strategies, tactical and operational changes to IT services through standardized procedures. The goal of change managent is to control risk and minimize disruption to IT service and business operations. So, IT industry, the process change management maturity model presents five levels of organizational maturity in change management: The five level may include: from the lowest level 1 to the highest level 5, level 1: Absent or Ad hoc, level 2: Isolated projects , level 3: Multiple projects, level 4: Organizatinal standards and level 5: organizational competency. So, for IT , software manufacturing industry, if the management knows how to manage and change software manufacturing quality in order to satisfy manufacturing organization can follow software users' needs to change old function to new function and improve their qualities to achieve the highest level 5 organizational competency level.

Then, I believe that due to this organization's software management can learn how software user needs change and change its any kinds of software functions (software life cycle), when its all softwares can be often changed to more new functions to create many different kinds of new software functions to satisfy software users needs and fight its software competitors in this often changing needs market. Due to software product may experience often changing life cycle stages. So, for often one learning software manager example, I believe that he can help this software organization to reach growth life cycle stage, even mature life cycle stage more easily in short time as well as he can also help his software organization to stay in mature life cycle stage long time if this software organizational manager can keep learning attitude to continue to create any new kinds of different functions software to satisfy software clients' changing needs for long time . Then, I believe that this software organization may experience or reach growth life cycle stage, even mature life cycle stage as well as continue staying long time on mature life cycle stage or avoid to encounter decline life cycle stage occurrence chance, if this software organization's softeare management can learn how to change software organization operation and software manufacture and sale strategy in order to satisfy this software users' needs in this software users' need often changing market . So, it is one example to explain why it has close relationship between learning organizational management method and business life cycle stages. As this software organization case, the software management needs often to create and change any new kinds of software functions in order to satisfy software users' needs . So, the software managers need to spend time to learn software life cycle stage , it can help the software organization may reach products life cycle stage, even mature life cycle stage in short time,even the software product organization may also stay long time in mature life cycle stage , when it can reach this stage. Hence, learning how to change organizational management or strategy, which is one important factor to help any organization can reach growth or mature life cycle stage eadily in short time.

As Lewin describes that the change as a three stage process of unfreezing, change and freezing . In this phases of change model, Lewin emphasizes that change is that a series of individual processes, but rather one that flows from one process to the next . So, in general, services mature firms pace greater emphasis on more bureaucratic form, control systems might need to change throughout the life cycle to fit in with. He explains they have relationship between both organizational life cycle stage and management control.

Effective management control may help the organization to reach mature life cycle in short time rapidly. So, leadership managment and the way of thinking are required to balance control and through several stages of growth, maturity , decline or re-grow changes in the external environment influence. Hence, managers position in each of the stages of life cycle and providing practical solutions are, however world where environment changes have proven a rapid growth, the management of varios , they also need to implement how to change their organizational cultures, strategies in order to let their organizations to reach mature stage with a distinction-oriented rapidly. Hence, to successfully implement change initiatives, for each phase of life cycle. Any organizations need to produce resistance to change (the old model wins out over management boils down to improving the relationship) learning the relationship between leadership style and the organization life cycle were important. The change from one organizational life cycle phase to another, it depends on how the manager'c capacity to learn and change.

However, organizations at any stage of the life cycle are impacted by external environment, for example, threats in the start up stage differ from those in the maturity stage. So, managers must need often to learn when the right time is to be needed to change the goals, instead he also needs to learn types of changes in the maturity stage, comparisons with other, having strong personal and professional relationships in the organizaton's maturity stage. Hence, I believe that it has close relationship between learning change management and reaching maturity life cycle and staying long time in this stage.

● How to achieve the experience of mature life cycle reaching stage rapidly for product and service ?

Any businesses expect they can have chance or possibility to attempt to experience this nature life cycle stage, but it is not guarantee any kinds of businesses must may experience this the topest stage, the question is that: Have any methods may help any kinds of businesses to reach this the topest level of business life cycle, when their businesses had been developing or expanding in a period, e.g. after five years? So, it has no absolute to guarantee any kinds of businesses must may experience this the topest stage in one fixed time. How businesses can adapt to birth and growth life cycle stages in order to reach this the topest mature stage in their business life cycle stages? I shall attempt to explain whether it is possible that achieving what strategies may help businesses bring high successful chance to reach the business life cycle mature stage as below:

Product life cycle with maturity stage, it foucs as an important strategic inflection point. A number of techniques can help their businesses to attempt to reach this stage more easily. In fact, the product life cycle contains four distinct stages: introduction, growth, maturity, and decline. Each stage is associated with changes in the product's marketing position . Any firms can use various marketing strategies in each stage to try to proplong the life cycle of their products.

How do the firm extend the maturity stage of a product? I shall recommend change price , place or promotion extension strategy , what does change price extension strategies mean? Change prices mean proces can be lowered to allow ew customers to buy it as well as change place means that products can be sold in different countries or territories to gain more sales, change promotion means different advertising or sales promotion techniques can proplong the life of the product, giving it a new image. So, any organizations can attempt to achieve this extension strategies in order to adapt in different birth, growth and maturity stages for ther product sale easily. This extension strategies' characteristics is at the product;s price, sold places and promotin methods can be changed in order to adapt clients needs when their products are selling in birth, growth and maturity three stages in order to achieve the most effective sale effort and clients growth increasing for long time.

In fact, any product is like human beings, products also have a limited life-cycle and they pass through several stages in their life cycle. A typical product moves through five stages, namely, introduction or birth, growth, maturity or saturation and decline stages. So, when the product needs the maturity life cycle stage, in this maturity stage, it has these characteristics: The maturity stage of the product life cycle shows that sales will eventually peak and then slow down. During this stage, sales growth has started to slow down, and the product has already reached widespread acceptance in the market, in relative terms, utimately, during this stage, sales will peak . Hence, any businesses ought need to consider what key strategies can be implement to achieve the best sale performance throughout the different product life cycle stages and how to make the most of each stage. For example, when the product is selling in the birth stage, e.g. one author's book , his book is selling to the publisher in the first year, there are not many readers knew this book existence, so this book is not popular, its price ought not change high to compare similar topic book, e.g. story book in this year, but after this year, if there are many readers know this book and readers number can grow up rapidly. This author's this topic story book does not change, either increases or decreases , but its sale number has been significant increasing after the first year . So, this author's this story book ought be raised book price to attempt to sell easily. It is one good example of extension strategy to this author's this story book in its life cycle stages. So, such as ths publisher book sale case, it may attempt to achieve extension strategies to every author's book sale, it can follow every author's book prices, publishing places and promotion methods to help every author to sell in the most competitive book sale price, sale place choice and promotin methods in order to earn their readers growth aim . So, any book , it is as product to book shop, it will experience introduction, growth, and maturity life cycle stages. Some books may attract many readers to consider or some books may not attract many readers to consider to read . So, it causes their reading life cycle stages staying time will be different. So, extension strategies can help any books to be sold easily.

In fact, instead of product has life cycle stage, any service also has life cycle stage. There are five stages in service lifecycle. Thay may include: Service strategy, service design, service transition, service operation and continual servce improvement five stages. The service strategy phase of the service lifecycle provides guidance on how to design , develop and implement service management. Because any service business needs to manage to any employee service performance in order to provide excellent service quality, e.g. property management service to building tenants or property owners , if the peoperty management furm can train employees to provide excellent property management service to let their managing building clients to feel satisfactory. Then, the property management firm ought may keep long time property management service to this building. So, service provider will also experience service performance different stages.

In different service performance life cycle stages, such as this property management service case, they ought implement dfferent strategies in order to let their employees to know how to achieve service performance improvement to let their servicing building clients (tenants or builgin owners) can feel their property management service can be continue improved to avoid to choose any property management service provider to replace it easily. The purpose of the service strategy stage of the service life cycle is to define the perspective, position plans and pattern that a service provider needs to be able to execute to meet an organization business outomes. The objective of service strategy may include: An understandng of work strategy is thus either the concept of the product life cycle or the concept of the service life cycle is today at about to give a propsed new product or service , how and to what extent. This generally requires important changes in marketing strategies and methods, because any learning kinds of service or product lif cycle stage why and how to change to any organizational management, it may be an important tool for marketers, managers, and product and service providing designers alike, If specifies four individuals stages of a product's or service's life and offers guidance for developing strategies to make the best use of these stages and promote the overall success of the product or service in the marketplace.

Reasons managment needs to spend time to learn how to manage his/her product or service life cycle development stage? They may include: The product or service life cycle is determined by how long its marketable . Product or service life cycle also plays a critical role in marketing strategy . So, learning how to adapt your product or service to meet the coming trends , this is the stage what will occue in which differentiation when the kind of the product or service will have possible to reach the another new experience life cycle stage in order to adapt its business development more easily.

Hence, each stage is associated with changes in the product's or service's marketing postion . The organizational management can use various markting strategies in each stage to try to prolong the life cycle of your products or services . Any product or service reaches the marketplace, it enters the service or product life cycle . This product cycle typically has for stages: Introduction or birth, growth, maturity and decline (and possibly deaths stages for product as well as service strategy stages includes service strategy. service design, servic transition, service operation, and continual service stages four service stages. So, the organization management can spend time to learn how to develop its business product or service needs to change in order to adapt marketing change in its product or service different life cycle stages. It can bring these benefits, such as: true benefits of product or srvice life cycle management may include, reduced time to makret, reduced market entry costs, more efficient and profitable distribution challen, higher return on investment from promotional cappaigns in possible, extending the lifetime of your product or service by adapting your approach as it moves through the lifecycle , for example, any management needs to learn what can make its products or services move from growth to maturity. After the introduction and growth stages, a product or service passes into the maturity stage. IN the first two stages , companies try to establish a market and then grow sales of their product or service to achieve as large , a share of that market as possible. Hence, marketers must be sure that a product or service has moved from one stage to the next before changing its marketing strategy. At each stage, marketing strategy varies. Strategy for the different stages of the product or service life cycle strategies may include: such as more benefits may be provided to the customers, e.g. extending the warranty period, guarantee period etc. However, company's market strategy depends on which stages the product or service is in its life cycle, for example, when one software manufacture company expects to expand its software sale market to overseas from local in growth stage. If it expects that it can reaches maturity stage in short time rapidly. It needs to implement technology innovation strategy for competition advantage reasons in global software sale markets development. Thus, the software organizational manager needs to spend time to learn what its present organizational characteristics are what resources and skills it owns or lacks, that gives it to comparative advantages over different countries to the operating changes that result in the learning curve to prepare this software product sale organizational maturity life cycle stage development more successfully. So, it needs to look at the advantages of focusing on what kinds of software manufacture and sale services in this software development industry whole life cycle stages and find the best or the most suitable competitive straregy, e.g. a discountinuous change to the software product development marketplace, what the global software product development industrial stage is and the tertiary or sale services sector durig the maturity life cycle stage to this softare manufacturer and sale organization strategy to this software firm during this growth stage may include example of it how changed its software product sales channels to which countries will be its another expanding sale market choice.

On conclusion, any organization management ought spend time to learn whether which strategies are the most suitable or the best to implement as well as how to implement when it is experiencing in the prodiuct or life cycle stage in order to spend less time to reach the maturity life cycle stage and proplong its maturity life cycle stage more success.

Human Behavioral network job brings social economic benefits

What does human network job mean ? Why may human network job be popular? Why human network job behavior may influence economy ?

Nowadays internet is popular to use. We can apply internet to find data , search any new things, even earn money. Why does internet

may become huma network job source. For example, e-publish may be one kind of new human network job. Any authors may apply internet channel to help them to sell electronic or paper books from e-publisher web store. They may apply facebook, you tub etc. any online

channel to promote themselves new books to let new readers to know whether when they may buy themselves favourable new topic books to read

from electronic publisher web store.

Thus, future electronic publisher industry may help any authors to build internet network platform to help them to sell and promote

ot advertise their any one new electronic or paper book topic to let global any one reader to choose to buy their any new topic books from electronic publisher web store easily and conveniently. However, it implies that electronic network platform author may be one kind of future new human network job in our societies.

How electronic network platform author job may bring economy benefit in macro economy view? A person can have few friends, contacts and still be very influential if these few

friends and contacts are themselves highly influential, e.g. one author must not need to know any one reader in global society. When they like to choose any electronic books from electronic internet network platform. They may become the author's any one topic book buyer, when they feel the author's any one topic book is fun and attract they make decision to buth the strange author whose the topic book from electronic book publisher's platform web store conventiently in short time. Although, they are strangers, they do not know themselves , but the reader can understand what it way that made Google from writing platofrm to create new creative mind and typing network job method to replace traditional hand writing book method for global authors. It will be one kind of new human network writing job.

Hence, global any one reader can apply an innovative search engine , such as google.com to find whether whom author personal new topic books are value to read from internet.

Then, the electroniuc publisher's web store may be new book store platform sale network to help the author to sell many electronic or paper books from electronic network platform

in short time. So, internet may be future new network plaform to help global any one author to create network writing job absolutely. Furthermore, internet may be popular social media

to help any one author to build goold relationship between his/her readers. It is one kind of new network, human network job. New authors do not need to buy many paper books to prepare to put in any one book shop warehouse. Their every book can print on demand to reduce out of book stock in any one book shop. They may choose to sell either electronic books or paper books both from any one book publisher web store. So, electronic network platform may be one kind of good writing channel to help human authors to create income and it can also help authors to bring new creative mind and new topic fun content books to let readers to know and buy to read from electronic publisher network platform.

Why does human behavior may be one kind of new human network job to bring global economic advantages. ALthough, it may be free income or without inocme, but the person does the network behavior, his/her behavior may be bring advantages to influence many other people's health. For this case, when a worker in a coffee shop in an airport gets a vaccination againnst the flu, it does not only helps him or her stay healthy, but also helps the many travellers who might otherwise have been inflected if that workers caught the flu. So, the externality , the result implies the vaccination of even a part of a community conveys benefits to the whole community. For example, governments pay special attention to the vaccinations of school children, teachers, health mothers, and the elderly, categories of people particularly susceptible not only to catching, but also to transmitting a disease.

It is not accidental that governments are heavily involved with vaccination . When there are externalities, free market, fail to persuade individual incentives with society's

their the worker's decision of whether to get a vaccine ends up attracting whether other people get sick. The workers might not fully take all these other people's potential suffering into account when making her or his vaccination decision.

As Stanford University does many suggestions, understand this and tries to help them make the right decisions and so providers free flu vaccines for its staff and students.

Small pockets of unvaccinated individuals can allow a disease to gain a spread more widely well-being. For example, parent weighing the costs and benefits of a vaccine for their child is not always thinking of the consequences of that vaccination to other people. THese are markets in which subsidizing or regulating behavior can make everyone better off. Because the reason for requiring that a child be vaccinated before enrolling in school is not just to protect that child, because each child's vaccination affects others via potential contagions.

Robots take our jobs behavioral and economy influences

Robot job behavior brings economy influences

If one day robots can replace human to do simple, even complex jobs. They will bring what influences to our global societial economy.The popular economic refrain declares that the

global middle class is dying and robots will soon take our jobs, e.g. shopping center customer service jobs, library service jobs, cinema ticket sale jobs, restaurant kitchen cooker jobs,

even, bus drivers, taxi drivers etc. public transport driving jobs, accountant, doctors etc. professional jobs. Whether it is beautiful or petty matter if our future societies have many human jobs can be replaced to do from robots. Businessman must may reduce to employ employees and reduce to pay salary or wage, when robots can be replaced to do their employees tasks. But, societies must bring unemployement rate rises , due to societies will have many people loss jobs when their employers choose to buy robots to serve their clients or do any office tasks or customer service or cleaning etc. tasks.

In micro economy view, employers may save money in long term, but in macro economy view, it will cause unemployment ratio rises , even crime rate rises when there are many people lose

jobs in societies. These models of doom, though, fail to account for the hundreds of businesses riding the waves of change in their industries when robots may be invented to replace human to do many simple , even complex tasks in our future societies.

WE may image that one small factory needs to manufacture fishes canes to sell to supermarket, the small , cheaper stuff and higher margin parts of the fishes manufacture industry. Before, this factory needs to employe many human factory workers need to help every fresh customer makeing the perfect fishing gear, designed for performance, durability, and cost in order to achieve to manufacture every fish cane in whole fished processing manufacturing stages. Every worker needs to spend about 15 to twenty minutes to finish every fish cane , till to delivery to any supermarket to sell. If this fish canes manufacturing factory can apply manufacturing robots to help them to finish any one working tasks , every robot can only spend five minutes to finish whole fresh fish cane manufacturing process. Thus, every robot can

help this factory save 10 to 15 minutes time to finsh every fish cane manufacturing process. IN fact, time is money, because when every robot can help this factory to reduce 10 to 15 minutes time to compare human worker. Then, this factory can finish about 20 fish canes in one hour if it can use robot to help it to manufacture fish canes. Otherwise, if this factory still use human workers to help it to manufacture fish canes, then it can finsh about 3 to 4 fish canes in one hour. SO, the manufacturing efficiency ensures that robots must help this fish manufacturing factory to raise fish canes number more than human workers. So, in robotic behavioral economy view, manufacturing robots must help this fish canes manufacturing factory to raise fish canes manufacturing number and deliver increasing number to supermarkets to prepare to sell every day. Robots can help this fish canes manufacturing factory bring manufacturing time saving, rising manufacturing efficiency, improving performance and reducing wages expenditure long time advantages in micro economy view. However, manufacturing robots can also bring disadvanages to society, e.g. increasing unemployment ratio, increasing crime rate,

this factory workers will lose jobs and income, they need earn social welfare from government and increasing government finance pressure in short time, even long time in macro economic view.

Stanford University graduate program in economics, Scott lecturer explained that "in demand and supply economic theory for robots supply and demand case, robots supply number increasing may influence human workers demand number decrease. It sometimes calls " the efficient frontier".

No specific human beings were mentioned in any of economics classes. As robots supply and demand in market case, They (robots) may be purely theoretical " agents" who reached to the most reasonable sale prices in order to persuade any one businessman buyer to make manufacturing robot buying decision whether robots can help him / her to bring how much saving time , saving money, saving cost, improving performance, efficiency economic benefit before he/she plans to reduce workers number when he/she decides to apply robots to replace human workers in his/her factory or office or any service department, e.g. cinema ticket sale service, shopping center customer service, shopping center cleaning , supermarket customer service etc. service or sale tasks. When robots can replace human to do any one of these tasks in any organizations. So, robots may be human worker agents who reached to prices the way robots would react to a software

command. There was nothing that explained why some people thrived and others did n't or why truly brilliant, hardworking people could fail when much lazier folks succeeded." Having been admitted to the Stanford University graduate program in economics, Scott lecturer hoped to get his answers there.

How robots influence our future social changing? Using the right technology can be a boon to your business in this economy. For internet example, it is easier than ever to find well-matched customers all around the world, to stay in contact with them, and to more quickly design the products they want. If you focus solely on being cutting -edge, though you risk letting the technology

take over what should be very robust relationships with your customers , employees, and colleagues. IN nowaddays society, technoligical advances and cutomation, personal

relationships in business are more crucial than ever. I mean that robots can not replace human to serve clients to let them to feel more comfortable and passion more easily. For shoe shop case example, if the shoe shop apply one robot to serve its clients to replace human shoe salesperson to serve its shoe customers. Robots ensure that they can not persuade every shoe potential buyer to make shoe buying decision more easily when robots need to contact every shoe potential buyer. The reason is simple, because robots can not touch any one shoe buyer individual emotion very easier.

If the shoe buyer needs the robots to help him/her to choose any right shoe styles when he/she can not feel himself / herself can make the most right shoe style choice decision. The robots can not replace human shoe salesperson to make shoe style choice judgement more easily. They must need longer time to analyze whether which shoe style may be the most suitable to the shoe buyer. Otherwise, human shoe salesperson may attempt to make the most right shoe style choice decision to help any one shoe buyer to chooce the most right style shoe because he/she owns shoe style sale experience, shoe style knowledge, the most important reason is that they can feel every shoe customer individual emotion to touch whether he/she will feel comfortable or happy when they attempt to help every shoe customer to seek the most right shoe style in every shoe customer whole shoe searching processing. Othwerwise, serving robots are only one machine, they can not touch or feel every shoe customer individual emotion whether he/she feel comfortable or unhappy or happy when they need to contact them in whole shoe searching processing. Hence, I believe that some tasks robots can

not repalce human staff to do very easily. Otherwise, robots may bring disadvanatges to let any one businessman to loss his/her customers, due to robots can not touch every customer

emotion to compare human staff in service tasks more easily. Robots serving customer behaviors may cause money lose and customers number lose to the shop in micro economic view.

Intellectual human economic behaviors

What does intellectual human economic behaviors mean ? I believe that when we choose or decide to do intellectual behaviors, then our societies will be influenced to bring economic growth in consequence.I shall attempt to indicate pollution case to explain how and why eithet our intellectual or foolish behaviors may bring economic growth or recession in consequence as below:

On one hand, for air pollution social case aspect example, if we only consider to buy cars to drive for working aimr or holiday leisure aim. Then, our societies air will be polluted. Our health will be influenced to bad. Our car driving behaviors may cause global environment air pollution serously. In long tiem, global air pollution will bring our bodies health to be bad. Although, ourselves car driving behaviors may bring our driving travelling leisure enjoyment and comfortable feeling in short time, also we so not need to pay public transport fare often, but we need to compensate ourselves health economic intangible loss due to air pollution , when cars number increases, dirty air will cause ouselves health to become bad.

In the result, we will need to pay more medical expenditure when we are old age, due to ourselves bodies will become bad, due to we breathe global dirty air every day, due to ourselves cars pollute air in long time, e.g. 10 to 20 years, even 30 more without limited air pollution environment. So, driving cars behavior may be one kind of human foolish behavior and our foolish behavior may bring ourselves future long time medical expenditure absolutely.

One the other hand, water pollution social aspect, if we often keep much rubblish to pollute sea, oil exploration porcessing pollute ocean , ships gas pollute ocaen, then fishes will eat polluted food and drive dirty water, due to global ocean is polluted.

In fact, because human only to conside how to buy boats to carry on leisure enjoyment activities, or catch cruises to travel on the sea. Also, oil manufacturers only consider researching anywhere to find new oil exploration places to manufacture oil product, when their oil exploration processes pollute ocarn . Consequently, global fishes drink polluted warer or eat polluted food. They will have poison. SO, human will have high chance to eat poison polluted fishes, due to fishes are poison or are polluted.

So, human is doing foolish activities, we only hope to find oil exploration places to pollute ocean or we only spend money to buy ticket to catch ships to travel anywhere in global ocean. All of these human foolish behaviors will bring pollution to global ocean. On consequently, we will need to compensate to eat polluted or dirty or poision fishes, ourselves bodies health will be bad. In long time, we need have high chance to pay medical expenditure when we are old. So, pollution case may be one good example to explain how and why human foolish behavior may influence ourselves future need to compensate serious medical loss.

All of these human foolish behavior will bring pollution to global ocean. On consequently, we will need to compensate to eat polluted or dirty or poison fished , ourselves bodies health will be bad. In long time, we will have high chance to pay medical expenditure, when we are old. So, pollution case may be one good example to explain how and why human ourselves intellectual or foolish behaviors may influence future long time economic loss or economic growth or recession in micro and micro economic view.

On another water pollution aspect hand, if we often keep rubbish to sea, oil exploration processing pollutes ocean and ships' gas pollute ocean, then fishes will eat polluted food and drink dirty water, due to fishes will eat polluted food and drink dirty sea water because the global ocean is polluted seriously.

In fact, because human only consider how to buy boats to carry on any leisure water activities, or catches cruises to travel on the sea. Also, oil manufacturers only consider any where to find oil exploratin places to manufacture oil products from ocean, when their pol exploration processes can plooute ocean. Consequently, global fishes drink polluted water or eat direty food. They will have poison. So, human will have high chance to eat poison fishes.

Otherwise, such as pollutin case, it can infuence inflation or deflation. Consequently, the reason indicates supply and demand theory. If air pollution is serious, then we will consider health issue, global cars demand number may be influenced to reduce, when global cars number demand will reduce, global car prices and supply number will need to change to fall down in order to attract or persuade global car consumers choose to make car purchase decision.

Hence, global car manufacture number and car price will be influenced to reduce, due to global air pollution issue. Consequently, deflation will occur because when the country citizen usually does not spend much extra saving money to buy car expensive goods. Money value will be low. Otherwise, if global cair pollution is not serious, human considers to buy cars to enjoy driving leisure lives. So, global car demand is influenced to increase , also global car price will also influenced to increase.

Consequently, gobal human will choose to buy cars to drive. Due to we accept to spend extra saving to buy expensive car goods. Car sale price and supply may be influenced to rise up. Money value is influenced to reduce. Inflation may be influenced, due to global car consumers number increases, we would not have extra money to spend easily. Car expensive goods expenditure influences our spending habit to avoid to make car purchase decision more easily. So, human intellectual or foolish activities may bring inflation or deflation consequency in possible indirectly in macro economic view.

On conclusion, above pollution case explain that how and why human intellectual or foolish economic behaviors may bring inflation or deflation consequency as wll as economic growth or recession consequency as well as any goods demand and supply increasing or decreasing consequency. It implies that human behavior may have indirect relationship to influence any goods demand and supply number to either increase or decrease result as well as any goods price will be influenced to increase or decrease in micro and macro economic view.

The relationship between social change and human behavior

Why does economic changes may influence human individual behavioral change? I shall attempt to indicate shopping behavior and staying at home behavior to explain their case and effect relationsip as below:

Human behavior can be influenced by economic change or economic change can be influenced by human behavior? Why does recession may influence consumers reduce shopping desire? In social recession suitation, it is possible that many people lose jobs suddenly, due to businessmen lose many customers. They need to make decision to reduce employees number in order to continue to keep businesses. Consequently, many firms (organizations) their employees may lose jobs. When they have much time, due to lose jobs, they will feel to avoid to spend too much time and money to go to shopping often. Many losing jobs people, they will often stay at homes.

So, they will reduce time to go to shopping, then non essential products won't their preferable choice purchase products. Hence, recession will change many losing jobs people their shopping or consumption desires to avoid to buy non essential products often . Usually when economic boom, many people have jobs to do because consumers number must increase when many people have jobs to do. Then, many people can accept to spend money to buy non essential products often. Many people feel spend time to go to shopping can satisfy their purchase of any kinds of new products useful psychology or desire. So, recession is one good example to explain it can influence many people do not like often to leave homes to go to shopping easily. Many people like to stay at homes, becaue they feel worry about spending too much shopping time when they leave homes. Their staying home time is one good negative shopping behavior example. So, economic change may influence human individual behavior changes , they have direct cause and efect relationship in behavioral economic view.

May human behavior influence economic change? Is it possible that human behavior may bring the country social economic change in macro economic or micro behavioral economic view ? I shall indicate publishing industry example. Do you feel that if there are many students feel learning is very important when they read many books or many of students feel interesting to read or they have reading new books in habit, then it is possible that the country will have many students like to spend time to go to any book shops to choose the books, they feel that they can help they learn new knowledge. Then the country will increase students number, they often spend time to visit any one book shop every week. Their visiting book shops behavior which may become their habits. So, the country will increase students number, they often spend time to visit book shops. Also, it implies that visiting book shops behaviors may be their behavioral habits.

So, when the country has many students often spend time to visit book shops , their visiting book shops behaviors may help any one book shop to raise books sale chance. So, the country's student individual often visiting book shop behaviors, their habitual visiting book shops behaviors must may assist help any one book shop to increase books sale number absolutely.

Consequently, any one book shop , its books sale bumber must be influenced to increase to increase because the country will have many students like or feel need visit book shops habit in order to choose any suitable books to buy to read at home in order to raise themselves learning effort. When the country has many bok shops often have many students visit their book shops, then their books sale number may be influenced to increase. It explain why student individual visiting book shop behavior may help any one book shop sale number increases also.

How human productive behavior may influence economic development

May any country which citizen behavior assist themselves country development? It is one cause and effect economic question. I mean that if the country itself citicen can not concentrate mind or energy to choose to do one kind of industry in order to let themselves country can bring the most benefit, then whether the counry itself economy can bring the most serious economic benefit. I shall attempt to indicate these countries themselves indistry choice to explain whether these countries themselves citizen productive behavior may help themselves countries to achieve the largest economic benefits. I shall indicate as below:

New Zealand farmer individual wine productive behavior

For New Zealand country example, this country concerns itself effort is foucs on farming agricultural aspect. So, this country has many farmers concentrate on farming agricultural aspect. May New Zealanders choose to spend time to produce different kinds of wines, e.g. wine or red grape wine is for the people are eating meat, or they are eating dinner.

When these New Zealanders their behaviors choose to do farming or agriculture to grow and produce different kinds of taste of white or red grape wine drinking products job. Themselves grape agriculture behavior will influence these New Zealanders themselves, they can learn how to improve different kinds of grape wine drinking products in order to achieve every kinds of white or read grape wines taste improving aim during their white or red grape producing process.

Why can New Zealander every individual white or read grape wine producers improve their white or read grape wine taste more easily? In behavioral economic view, it can explain that why any one New Zealander white or read grape wine producer can be encouraged or excited or persuaded to concentrate nervous and energy and effort to learn how to improve their white or red grape wine products easily.

In fact, New Zealand is one agricultural food export country. It has good natural environment resource , e.g. land, seed to provide any one farmer to produce themselves any kinds of agricultrual food products, e.g. fruit, or wine food products. Because New Zealanders know themselves country has enough natural resource . So, in common, many New Zealanders choose to attempt to do farming agricultural jobs in order to export themselves any kinds of fruit or meat or wine products to overseas or sell to domestic in order to earn profit.

So, when these New Zealand farmers number has been increasing every year. This country farmers will feel themsleves competition between this New Zealand farmers themselves are serious due to they may feel New Zealanders choose to do agriculture businesses in order to export themselves different kinds of farming food to overseas or sell to local to earn profit.

Hence, when many New Zealand farmers feel that farmers number has been increasing every year. They will feel themselves competition is serious. They must need to spend much time and nervous and effort to research what method is the best how to produce the best taste of white or red grape wine products in order to let local or overseas wine buyers to choose to buy his/her producing white or read grpae products to drink.

Hence, in competition psychological view, may influence many New Zealand white or reaad wine producers had been beginning to change their learning behavior on researching what method is the best in order to produce the best quality of taste red or white wine products to sell in order to attract overseas or local white or read grape wine drinkers to choose to buy his/her wine products. Their behavior will focus on learning how to raising or improving white or read grape wine taste method more than only focus on producing a large number white or red grape wine products. They believe wine quality is more important to compare wine producing number. So, New Zealand wine producers themselves wine producers behaviors have been changing on concentrating on researching wine quality method aspect more then wine producing number aspect in behavioral economic view.

America high technological productive behavior

For America example, US is one high technological country, it owns many high technological knowledge talent inventors, e.g. computer science inventors. Hence, US must attract many diferent countries owning high technological computer inventors choose to go to US to develop their computer science profession career. Also, it seems that when many computer science inventors or professions choose to go to US to develop themselves computer science new career. In behavioral economic view, due to their leaving themselves countries choice, which may bring influence themselve country job behaviors need to be changed. They must need to adapt US new live. Because they will forgive their past computer science job. These computer science professionals need to spend time to adapt US new lives. They " past computer science job behaviors" will need to be changed to their new US any computer employer's new computer science job model.

Because their traditional computer science jobs needed to be forgot in their themselves countries. They will feel their old computer science job knowledge and behavior needed to change in order to let their US any one new of computer company employer feels satisfactory to accept their new working behavior in any one US computer organization.

So, on the other hand, many US computer company employer will feel that they must need time to accept any one new overseas computer science professions their working behaviors, their working attitude daily, because these foreign comouter science professional, their past computer working behaviors and working attitude must be different to US domestic computer science professions.

In behavioral economic view, these overseas computer science professions, their working behaviors and attitude must be needed to change in order to adapt any one US new computer company itself domestic or local computer science professional stafs themselves daily working behaviors and attitude because these overseas and local computer science professionals must need to team work together.

In behavioral economic view, it is only one way that foreign computer science professionals must need to change themselves past country traditiona daily working behaviors and attitude in order to cooperate with these US local computer science professionals in teams more easily.

Consequently, if these foreign compute science professionals can change their past working behaviors and attitude to let any one US local computer science professional feels to cooperate with them easily in short time. Then, the US computer company itself whole computer professional teams themselves efficiencies will be influenced to raised or improved by the changing past working attitude and working behaviors of these foreign computer science professionals. So, in behavioral economic view, only if US any one computer company hopes itself computer teams themselves efficiency can be raised or improved when it decides to employ foreign computer science professionals and US domestic computer science professionals. They need to work in teams together. They must need to let these foreign computer science professionals to know how to change their working behaviors and attitude to let their domestic computer science professionals feel easy to work together. Then, the US computer company itself whole team efficiency must be rasied or improved easily in short time.

- ● China share market investing behavior

For China share market example, economic development depends on financial market. Because if many Chinese have interest to invest to carry on shares buying and selling activities in orde to learn how to earn shares interest and share profit when the China shareholder can make decision to sell himself/herself shares in the the high price, then he/she can earn money when he/she can sell the China company's shares in the high sale share price position.

If China has many Chinese like to spend time to carry on investing shares activities. Themselves shares buying and selling behaviors will influence China has many companies can increase fund from many Chinese shareholders in order to have enough money to expand or develop themselves businesses in China in long term.

Consequently, when China can have many Chinese like to attempt to carry on buying and selling shares investing behaviors in China share market. Themselves buying and selling shares behaviors can help many Chinese companies have effort to increase enough money or capital in order to continue to do their businesses in long term absolutely. So, it explains why when many Chinese become shareholders , they can assist China will have many companies continue to develop their businesses if many Chinese like to carry on shares buying and selling investing behaviors in long time in China financial investment market nowadays in behavioral economic view.

Why has any individual country have many people invest share behavior which can influence the country's macro consumption desire?

I shall apply shares market buying and selling investment behavior to explaiin why shares investment behavior which may impact the country's overal consumption desire as below:

In behavioral economic view, I assume that when the coutry has many people have interest to attempt to carry on shares buying and selling investment behavior, then their frequent shares buying and selling behaviors which may bring negative consumption desire or shopping desire of these shares investors their consumer behavior.

The reason is simple, when the country has many share buyers number suddenly been increasing rapidly. Consequently, these large group share investors must need to spend much time to research any kinds of company shares variations, whether when their share prices will rise up of fall down in order to achieve buying the company's shares in the lowest price and selling the company's shares in the highest price level in order to earn profit.

Basic on this reason, they must need to spend much extra time to research share prices changing behavior every day, e.g. one working person will wait to leave his/her job, after he/she can spend time to gather data to research the day's share price changing behavior after dinner. So, the working person's right time may be his/her share price market research behavior. Before he/she may spend his/her night time to go to shopping after dinner, but nowadays, he/she will fogive to do his/her shopping behavior before dinner or after dinner at hight sometime. He/she will make decision to spend much night time to turn on computer to click on share market website to research his/her share purchase choice to investigate whether his/her share price whether it rises up or falls down at the moment in order to make his/her share buying or selling decision at ever night time.

I mean the when the country has many people are share investors, their shares investment behavioral spenging time which will influence many shops lose customers at might often because the country will have many people feel need to spend night time to turn on computer or watch television to investigate share price variation. So, the country will have many people / share investors choose to stay at home in order to carry on share price variation investigation behavior, they need to listen share market update news from radios or watch the share market update news from computer or TV at home every night. Consequenly, they must reduce times to leave themselves homes at night. So, their shopping behavior also will be reduced. Because these share investors feel need to spend time to investigate share price variation news at homes which can bring economic benefits (high opportunity benefits) when they choose to forgive to leave homes to go to shopping times (opportunity cost) every night.

On conclusion, it seems that when the country has many people are share investors, then their share price investigating behavior may bring negative shopping emotion at night. Consequently, the country's any one shop may lose many customers from this share investor consumer group in behavioral economic view. Hence, when the country's share investors number had been increasing rapidly, it will influence any shops lose many customers from this share investing customer group at night frequenly in short time, even long time in behavioral economic view, because their shopping desires or shopping emotion will be brought negative feeling when they make decisions to spend much time to listen radios or watch TV or computers share price update nes at night. Hence, share market will bring negative impact to influence consumer shopping desire or negative shopping emotion in behavioral economic view.

Can technology influence human shopping behavioral change?

Nowadays, technological development has reached mature stage, whether technological mature stage may bring positive or negative shopping emotion influence to global consumers. I shall aplly internet inventin or ecommerce shopping channel tool to explain whether internet technology can bring postive or negative influence to global consumer behavior in behavioral economic view.

Internet is a good technological tool, it brings e-commerce business chance. In fact, commonly, global has have many businessmen choose to use internet channel to carry on their products transactions between global online-buyers and their electronic websites. So, global many shoppers had begun to feel online shopping is more convenient to compare visiting shops shopping. Their shopping behaviors have been changed from internet technological tool. Global has many shoppers choose to buy any products from any overseas or local businessmen their web stores. They only need to spend time to find any businessmen their webstores to choose the most suitable products to pay visa to buy from their webstores. at homes. So, in general, global had have may shoppers had changed their shopping behaviors from visiting shops to visiting webstores at homes often.

So, it seems that internet technological tool had influenced global many shops disappear, but internet webstores will be replaced their actual shops on streets. Some of businessmen either they choose webstores to replace shops or choose websotes and shops both or still keep shops only. Hence, internet tool influences global businessmen have three kinds of products sale channels to let globa local and overseas consumers to choose how to buy their products. However, in fact, many of global shoppers, youngers and olders had begun to accept to buy any products from webstores. They feel to spend time to leave homes to visit shops , their shopping behaviors will be wasted time to not essential part to their daily lives. Hence, since internet technological invention, it had changed many consumers their traditional visiting shops shopping habit to change to buying products from webstores channel.

However, on the one hand, internet creates webstores ecommerce shopping channel to let global many consumers do not need to leave homes to go to shopping. It brings negative visiting shops shopping emotion to global general consumers nowadays. But on the other hand, it also brings positive visiting internet webstores shopping emotion to global general consumer nowadays. So, it seems that global many consumers feel that they often do not need to spend much time to go out shopping. Many global consumers feel convenient and enjoy to choose any products to buy from different internet webstores, when the online buyer chooses the most suitable product, he she only needs to pay visa card to buy the product from the online seller's webstore conveniently at home.

Hence, online shopping can bring economic benefit to online buyers, e.g. avoiding walking time or spending transport fare to visit the shop to go to shopping, shortening or reducing shopping time to do another important matter.

On conclusion, global many consumers began feel online shopping can bring more economic benefits on shortening shopping time, avoiding transport fare spending aspect. So, online shopping will be popular shopping behavior for future long time. It may encourage global many shoppers can make rapid shopping decision in short time in order to carry on any products buying transaction to global any one online shopper in short time easily in behavioral economic view. So, global many businessmen had begun to build themselves one attraction webstore in order to persuade different countries consumers to choose to click themselves webstores from internet channel to buy any kinds of products in short time easily.

So, internet technology had changed consumers traditional shopping behaviors to build positive online shopping emotion as well as raise online sellers' any products sale chance easily in behavioral economic view.

Why and how human behavior may influence the country's economic growth or recession?

When one country has many people choose to do the same matter for one period, whether their behavior may influence the country's pvera; economic growth or recession . I shall attempt to indicate cases toexplain their relationship as below:

For flowing rubblish behavioral case example, do you feel that when the country has many people often flow rubblish on the streets, instead of their flowing rubblish behavior may bring streets dirty? But, their flowing rubblish behavior may explain that this country has people may have enough money to buy food to ear, or enough cloths to wear, enough bottles of water to drink, even they may have enough money to buy new television, radio, refrigeraters , washing machines, desktops or laptops electronic home products from old to new to use in order to satisfy their living needs. So, when they flow old electronic home products, their flowing old home electronic products behaviors may seem that they have enough money to buy other new home electronic products to replace old home electronic products to use at homes.

However, it seems thaat this country ought have many people have jobs to do. So, many of them, they can easy to make purchase decison to flow any old home electronic products and buy any new home electronic products to use . Because this country has many people have jobs to do. So, they can often not use old home electonic products to become rubblishs to flow on streets after they had bought any kinds of new home electronic homes.

In fact, it also implies that this country's economy grows rapidly. So, many businesses can glow up rapdly. When they expanded their businesses, they must need to increase employees number in order to let they help themselves to raise productivity or serve their clients absolutely. So, when the country has many businesses can grow up, it seems that its economy must be better or it is improved to compare past. Due to many different kinds of home electronic products had been often bought to use by this country people in this period. So, this country's any streets can be observed that expensive electronic home products were flowed on streets anywhere. then, this country will have many electronic home products sellers can sell their home electronic products very easily. When this country has many people can find any kinds of jobs to do easily. So, due to unemploymen rate had been decreasing.

In behavioral economic view, as this many electronic home products rubblish country case, we can observe this country may have many people have jobs to do. So, consumption number has been increased long time. So, cheap food, or expensive home electronic products may be rubblish on any streets. This country's people , their flowing rubblish behaviors may be explained that many of people have enough jobs to do, so they have ability to buy any good taste food to eat or buy any kinds of expensive electronic home products to use. So, this country's economy may be improved for this long period. So, in behavioral economic view, when this country can have many electronic home products rubblishs are flowed on anywherer in streets frequently. It seems that this country will have many people have jobs to do, so it causes they often change old home electronic products or replaced them easily, when they have enough income to spend to buy any kinds of new home electronic products to use at homes easily. Moreover, their flowing old electronic home products behaviors also indicate that this country has many people their salaries may be increased in possible from their emplyers. When this country can have many different kinds of home electornic products are sold. It means that this country's electronic home products needs or demand had been increasing, due to many people have jobs to do and income increases to excite their living of needs also improve. Consequently, this country may seem have better economic improvement. We can observe from this country's electronic home products rubblish increasing income in theis period.

On conclusion, this country ought experience economic growth at this period. So, " flowing expensive electronic home rubblish increasing number " may seem that this country's economic growth is rapidly in this period, due to many people have jobs to do as well as salaries increase in this period.

Technology how impacts human behavior changing?

Technology how influences human behavior to bring changing? For example, online share purchase and sale transaction from smart phone brings share investor can do share buying or selling transation in any where and any time conveniently, non manual driving auto vehicle, bring car owner feels comfortable and spends free time to do other matter, e.g. reading, listening mucis in himself or herself car freely. electrical energy vehicle can help car owner to reduce air polluton and it can brings the drivers do not feel drive long time in any journeys in order to avoid air pollution for environmental protection responsible car drivers in our societies. Thus, they will drive long time in any journeys when they can drive electronic energy cars to replace oil energy cars.

However, online technology can also bring consumers can choose to stay at homes to buy any things from seller individual online webstore conveniently. Such as online technology can bring shoppers do not need to spend much time to visit shops to buy any things. They can choose any kinds of products from any online sellers individual online webstores conveniently at homes. Online technology excite busy consumers can make purchase decision easily as well as it can help online sellers sell any kinds of products from internet easily.

In behavioral economic view, technology can change human behavior to be improved, it can let human feels comfortable, more free time ro use, rapid making any decisions, such as apply smart phones to make share purchase or sale transaction decision, online shopping decision, even travelling any where decision in short time, when the traveller finds the most cheap hotel accommodation room price and air ticket price frm any travel agent online tourism webstore, then the potential travel customer can follow the online hotel accommodation price and air ticket price data to make decision when to buy the air ticket from the airline travel agent or make decision when to prebook which hotel accommodation room to go to the country to travel from online travel agent tourism webstores. So, technology can encourage global any country travelers to make anywhere to trvel rapidly. If the traveler can find the country's general hotel rooms and airline tickets prices had been decreasing more sightly. The traveler may make travel decision to choose the country to travel in short time, then he/she can prebook the country;s any hotel room and airline ticket to pay by visa fraom the country's any hotel and airline travel agent webstores., before one week, even one month or more easily. Hence, online technology can also encourage traveler individual frequent travel times to be increased, due to global travelers can find any hotel rooms and airline tickets prices from internet conveniently at homes. They do not need to spend time to visit any airline travel agent to enquire travel choice country's hotel rooms prices and airline ticket prices. They can compare global travel of countries choices ' all hotels rooms and airline agents air tickets prices to make prebook airline seat and hotel room decision before one week, one month even six months early.

On conclusion, online technology can encourage global travelers can make travelling any where and when traveling time desicions easily. It can excite tourism industry develops in long time. Also, such as electricity cars invention can encourage environment protection car owners do car purchase decision easily, because they can choose to drive electronic energy cars to replace oil energy cars in order to avoid air pollution occurs easily. So, electronic cars can increase electronic car purchasrs number, due to many of environmental protection attitude of car owners can choose to drive electricity cars to bring air cleans, even non -manual driving cars can encourage lazy driving and free time driving car owners to choose to buy non-manual (artificial intelligent) cars to drive , because they can spend much free time to read, listen music or do any matters in themselves cars, they do not need to drive cars, robotic (AI) auto driving machine is such one non-manual driver to help them to drive themselves cars confidently. So, non-manual driving cars can attract lazy and enjoying free time driving car owners to choose to buy to replace traditional manual cars to drive easily. Moreover, online share transaction can help any share investors to make share buying and selling decision in short time easily. When they can apply smart phones technological tool to carry on share buying and selling activities easily. They can observe any share rising or falling price suitation from smart phones in any where any any time easily. So, smart phone technology can help global any shareholders to make share purchase and sale transaction easily. So, technology can encourage human makes decision in short time rapidly.

How and why employees behaviors may influence economy development?

In behavioral economy view,I believe the country's any organizational employees behavior may bring indirect relationship to influence the country's long term economic development. I shall indicate past manufacture industry social development period to explain their relationship. For many countries' past business activities had belonged to manufacturing industry, such as US, UK past before 1980 year, it focused on steel manufacturing and steel manufacturing related machine products. So, US, Uk developed countries manufacturing industries may be past main country's economic income sources. I assume US , UK past had one million number different kinds of industries. They ought had about seven houndred thousand number organizational businesses were belonged to manufactured industry. They may include:

Steel manufacturing and steel related machine manufacturing, e.g. vehicle manufacturing, home appliances, e.g. washing machine, television, radio, refrigerate cooler, heater, air condition etc. different kinds of different kinds of steel -related manufacturing machine, they were manufactured from US, UK steel machine manufacturers. So, US, Uk the other three hundred thousand number industry may be general service industry, e.g. hotel service, restaurent, cinema, public transport service, tourism lesiure , wine bar, supermarket etc. different kinds of non-manufacturing industries business organizations were operated in UK, US past before 1980 year.

So, in UK, US developed countries industry development history, they ought have high percentage of businesses belonged to steel related manufacturing machine and steel products. Also, in the past before 1980 year, US, Uk business employers , they employed many workers are manufacturing workers. They needed to spend long time to work in factories. They were skillful workers, and they are trained to manufacturing cars, washing machine, television, heater, etc. even steel itself different kinds of steel related products to prepare to deliver to their shops to sell to US, Uk local or overseas clients.

So, I believe that past UK, US ought employ many employees, they belonged to skillful manufacturing workers, manufacture increasing steel machine or steel related machine number of products rapidly daily. So, if UK, US had had many of these manufacturing factories owned high skillful workers, then their manufacturing steel-related machine or steel both kinds of products number must be influenced to raise rapidly. Consequently, their steel machine manufacturing products would been exported to overseas or would been sold to local both markets , they may be influenced to raise sale number. They (these manufacturing workers) needed to be trained to know how to manufactur these different kinds of machine products in the efficient teams and they ought to be trained to raise their efficiencies in order to shorten time to manufacturing many kinds of steel related manufacturing machine or steel itself products rapidly. So , if their efficiencies and manufacturing performance was improved, these US, UK any one manufacturing worker and their teams ought achieve raising productivities significantly.

Hence, when past UK, US manufacturing industry development period, if these two countries' any manufacturing factories could have many manufacturing workers could be trained to be skillful and proficient manufacturing workers. Then, in past every day to these factories workers, they ought help their steel or steel related manufacturing employers to raise any kinds of machine or steel products number in every team. So, when past in the manufacturing industry development, US, UK could have many factories' manufacturing workers themselves steel or steel related machine products manufacturing skill could be trained to to improve to any kinds of these machine or steel manufacuring products quality as well as their products number could be influenced to raise by themselves skillful improvement significantly every day.

Then, what would be influenced to occur to past UK, US manufacturing industry period? In behavioral economic view, when these two manufacturing industry developed countries, such as UK, US , if they had many factories workers can be trained to improve their skill in order to achieve any kinds of steel or steel-related machine products quality could be improved as well as products manufacturing number could be also increased absolutely.

In consequence, past UK and US both countries ought increase themselves any kinds of steel and steel related machine products number to be supplied to themselves local shops to let local clients to choose any one kind of machine manufacturing products to buy easily as well as they could also export to supply overseas any countries to buy their different kinds of steel or steel related machine products to let overseas steel or steel related manufacturing machine product buyers, they can have many of these different kinds of these steel or steel-related different kinds of manufacturing machine from UK and UK these both countries easily to compare other countries.

On conclusion, I believe that past US, and UK macro manufacturing industry income GDP would increase significantly. So, they would have good economic growth performance because when many of these manufacturing workers themselves manufacturing effort could be improved. So, it explained when employees manufacturing abilities can influence economic growth indirectly.

Robots invention whether they can help organizations to raise efficiencies or inefficiencies?

In behavioral economic view, in any organizations, when the organization hopes its worker teams can raise efficiencies , the organization may choose to increase more workers number and/or it can provide training to improve these workets themselves skills in order to raise their efficiencies. For one warehouse example, when the warehouse increases many goods , they are needed to delivered these goods from the shelves to the delivering destination locations. If this warehouse supervisors feel these workers themselves goods delivery speeds are slow, which is possible due to this warehouse's workers number is not enough. So, this warehouse supervisor ought increase workers number in order to increase their goods delivery speed in order to deliver goods from the shelves to every indicated goods delivery destination in order to let any one lorry driver can transport the right kinds of goods and ensure the accurate goods number to transport to any one client home rapidly.

However, if this warehouse supervisor planed to buy several warehouse goods delivery robots to assist these warehouse workers to find the right kinds of goods from shelves and then deliver to the right destination location in the warehouse. So, these warehouse orkers can concentrate on counting the accurate goods number and ensuring the right kinds of goods in order to prepare to let lorry drivers to transport these goods to these goods of buyers themselvers homes rapidly. Consequently, in the first step, robots can concentrate on finding th right goods from shelves and delivers them to the right goods transportation of location destination. Then, in the second step, these warehouse workers can concentrate on counting the accurate goods number and ensuring the right kinds of goods in order to prepare to put them to the lorry. Consequently, when warehouse robots and warehouse workers can cooperate to work together, the most important, robots, can deal on finding the right kinds of goods and deal on delivering the accurate number of goods of job duty as well as these warehouse workers can only concentrte on counting the right kinds of goods number in order to avoid it has none any mistake of wrong kinds of goods and inaccurate goods of delivery number to be transported to the lorry and to deliver to any one buyer's home.

So, it seems that warehouse robots ought help any one warehouse worker to raise himself efficiency and avoid goods delivery of mistake occurrence easily as well as their help to warehouse workers that can let any one goods buyer feels their goods can be delivered to their homes rapidly. Moreover, warehouse robots can also help these warehouse workers to raise efficiencies because warehouse robots can help them to shorten goods delivery time between any one shelf and any one goods delivery destination of location in the warehuse because robots may help them to find the right kinds of goods from the right shelf in the short time. So, any one worker does not need to spend long time to seek anywhere is the right shelf location for the kind of goods when the kind of goods are needed to deliver to the buyer's home from lorry. Warehouse robots can help them to do this aspect of " finding the goods from the right shelf in short time job duty". So, any one warehouse worker only needed tospend less time to do the counting of any right kind of goods number and ensuring the right kind of goods job duty. Consequently, this warehouse 's any one worker, his any one kind of goods delivery time may be reduced, because robots' assistance and they may have more confidence to avoid mistake to deliver the wrong number of goods and/or the wrong kind of goods to any one goods buyer's home.

On conclusion, it seems that warehouse robots ought may help any one warehouse worker to raise efficiency for any one team in the warehouse as well as the warehouse any one supervisor does not need to spend much time to observe any one worker individual performance for " goods delivery job duty aspect" because their goods delivery job duty that had been replaced to do by these several warehouse robots. Robots can achieve the more accurate of right kinds of goods and the right number of goods delviery job performance to compare any one of human warehouse worker themselves right kinds of goods of delivery and right number of goods of delivery job performance. So, when robots can participate to cooperate with this warehouse's any one worker to do their goods of delivery job duty in this warehouse every day. Then, robots can raies any one of supervisor individual confidence in order to let they do not need to spend time to observe any one of worker individual whose goods of delivery job performane. They can concentrate on supervising any one worker whose goods transport to lorry in the final step in order to avoid to deliver wrong goods number and / or wrong kind of goods to any one goods buyer's home every day. Consequently, this warehouse's overall teams of their delviery of goods performance many be improved by robotss' participatin to goods of delivery task as well as this warehouse's oveall teams themselves efficiencies may be influenced to raise by robots' goods of delivery task participation.

Why social behavior may influence organizational strategy needs to be changed ?

Why any organizations need to know whether nowadays social behaivor how has been changing in order to implement the kind of the most right strategy to achieve the profit aim pursue in possible. I shall indicate nowadays ecommerce or online, customer shopping behavior to explain above question concerns they ought have close relationship between social behavior and organizational strategic choice or organizational behavioral changing need. On nowadays ecommerce business, or online shopping model, this kind of shopping model in global many young and old age consumers like to apply internet tool to choose any country sellers website stores in order to stay at home to buy any kinds of products from themselves webstores in global societies.

In fact, online shopping model had been popular for long time above to twenty years. Most of global sellers will make decision to design themselves webstores in order to attract global many online buyers to choose to buy their products from themselves webstores. So, it seems that social consumers purchase behaviors had been changed to online shopping from internet invention.

Hence, social consumers purchase behavioral changes may influence any organizations' strategies need to be changed from visiting shops purchase strategy model to online purchase strategy model, if the seller still concentrate on concentrate on considerate how to design itelf , but neglects to considerate how to design itself webstore, e.g. how to design attract product photos to put on itself webstore, how to arrange sale price information location to be putted on webstore and visa card payment location on itself webstore in order to let any one online buyer can feel very easier to buy itself any kinds of products from itself webstore. Then, its potential online buyers will be influenced to increase number when they can find this online seller itself any kinds of products photes and every kinds of product sale price information and visa card payment channel locations easily from itself webstore.

So, it implies that nowadays any one seller ought need to design one webstore to let any one online overseas and domestic consumers can have chance to click itself webstore to choose any one kind of product to buy conveniently when he/she does not hope to leave him/her home to go to shop, because nowadays social shopping behaviors had been influenced to change when internet invention, them it gives another online purchase method to replace visiting shops purchase method to global any one buyer in nowadays societies.

So, if nowadays any one seller still concentrate on how to design itself shop display in order to put any kinds of product on shelf in order to let any one visiting shop customer to find the kind of product to buy, but it neglects to change to choose to pursue another new technological shopping method, such as webstore purchase method in order to implement effective strategy to design the most right webstore as well as in order to attract global overseas and local consumers to find itself webstore easily from website and find its any one kind of product phots and sale price and visa card payment button in order to choose to buy itself any kinds of products in the short time. Consequently

I believe that the seller will lose many customers from overseas and local when its other same or similar product sellers choose to design themselves webstores in order to let global any one product buyer can buy themselves any one kind of product when they can pay visa card to buy their products from them webstores conveniently when they stay at home habitly. Then, the seller will lose many global potential customers in long time.

On conclusion, in behavioral economic view, any consumer behavioral social changing, which will influence any in order to avoid customers number loses significantly . In future time, organizations need to make rapid decision in order to implement the most reasonable and the most useful strategy in order to avoid global potential customers number reduces or lose them in long time. So, social behavioral changing environment ought influence any global organizations need to decide how to change themselves strategies in order to avoid customers loses significantly in future time.

www.ingramcontent.com/pod-product-compliance
Lightning Source LLC
Chambersburg PA
CBHW081915120726
47996CB00010B/3334